CONTENTS

"It is the spirit that gives life, while the flesh is of no avail. The words I have spoken to you are Spirit and life. But there are some of you who do not believe."

JOHN 6:63

I think 99 times and find nothing. I stop thinking, swim in silence, and the truth comes to me.

ALBERT EINSTEIN

"Silence is the language of god, all else is poor translation."

RUMI

Amen, Amen, I say to you, he who believes in me (Jesus), will do the works that I do, and will do greater works than these.

JOHN 14:12

My brain is only a receiver, in the Universe there is a core from which we obtain knowledge, strength and inspiration.

NIKOLA TESLA

"The people who know God well – mystics, hermits, prayerful people, those who risk everything to find God—always meet a lover, not a dictator."

RICHARD ROHR, OFM

Foreword

This is NOT a typical book about spirituality! This is a story that can become a handbook of sorts for living life differently; that is, living YOUR life differently, to your benefit, regardless of who you are. In Richard Braconi's book, *Being More of God*, he strives to communicate his personal experiences of his spiritual journey such that all can benefit. What makes his story relatable is that he clearly states, with stark reality, the life-changing challenges he endured financially and how painful this was for him regarding his most cherished family relationships, his business, and his previous career. His fears and doubts are palpable, evoking a visceral response in readers, such that we can feel and appreciate the anxiety from many perspectives. However, the immeasurable rewards, as well, are vividly described as his progress is validated by ongoing incremental experiences that hold up to objective verification.

Rich's true story removes excuses as to why you, I, or anyone cannot and should not live a more spiritual life. Moreover, this story explains how and why we all can benefit from what each of us has unlimited access to, which is our spirit. The spirit in each of us has been just waiting; waiting to help us. Rich did not have a mentor through his journey, and by being alone, separate from his family during the early years of his journey, he drew upon and summoned more spirituality than he ever thought he'd had.

So, who am I to author this foreword? I had worked in clinical roles for almost a decade and later was at the top of my game in Financial Services after an additional three decades, and I was the biggest skeptic who was ready to disprove this idealistic, unfounded, woo-woo, "feel good" nonsense—until I tried it! If you have a scientific interest, business background, and/or base belief in facts, challenge yourself, as I did, to disprove the capability of spirit or of energy and how we are all connected. Regardless of whether verbiage refers to spirit, energy, or another term, Rich relates his story to clearly articulate and demonstrate what is universal.

We're all so busy trying to figure out life and how to master the next gadget, handheld piece of technology, market move, and so on, yet Rich shows us how we have the most amazing infinite source of personal energy or spirit that has been and is ready to help each of us realize more personal miracles and joy than we could have imagined.

Instead of constantly trying to outmaneuver the universe, try tapping into it for your own good and as part of a greater good! Rich shows the reader how to easily and incrementally try his approach with minimal to no risk in everyday situations. Dare yourself to be inspired!

MARYANN KELLY

B.S., R.T.R, Advanced Medical Intuition, Reiki, Light Grid, Energy Medicine

Preface

Only through our own sincere, willful
effort to seek universal truth will we be
divinely led to a more profound perspective
of ourselves.

The spiritual perspective I will be sharing throughout this book comes from knowledge that I was divinely inspired with while I sought to prove or disprove the existence of my own spirit, a unique communication within my spirit, and a universal God. My goal throughout this book is to break down the knowledge I have received throughout this journey into a simple, common-sense explanation of how a true source of divine intelligence that uses the power of unconditional love to communicate, does, in fact, universally coexist within us all.

Throughout this book I refer to the word "spirit" often. Spirit is any intelligent love-based self-evolving energy that can harmoniously exist within a physical form or without a physical form. People and animals are a "spirit" temporarily existing within a physical form. Commonly, it is not until our "spirit" disconnects or ascends from its physical form that we view ourselves as a "spirit."

This true story is about my search for an absolute truth of whether everyone has the same higher purpose in life—but with different opportunities and paths to achieve that purpose—and whether I was personally capable of receiving divine guidance to help me fulfill mine.

My spiritual awakening began approximately eleven years ago, at a time when I finally decided to make a sincere, willful effort to surrender all control and sole ownership over my life to a divine intelligence I refer to as God. During my spiritual search, I decided to use solely the outcome of my own experiences as a means of proving the existence or nonexistence of a universal God of unconditional love.

To significantly change my initial skepticism of being able to communicate with a godly intelligence required real-world, evidential proof. To accept that a universal loving God truly existed and I was truly a spiritual child of God, I felt that some kind of communication should naturally exist between God and me. And, if I had a proper understanding of how this communication works, I could use it to receive a more profound perspective of myself, which I would use to build a better life. In addition, if this more profound perspective was able to credibly unlock and prove abilities that are intrinsic to my own spirit as well as universally inherent to the respective spirits of others, then the source of this higher education would definitely be God to me.

I was at a rather low point in life when I courageously committed to accepting only the truth regardless of the results that commitment might bring about. I chose to challenge the validity of all my prior beliefs, such as those from my Catholic upbringing as well as beliefs imposed by family and friends, by my schooling, and by society. However, I was not under any illusion that just because I was seeking and wanted divine help, my life would suddenly be blessed and be problem free through some sort of divine intervention.

My story details how I managed to abandon the self-destructive path I had been on and choose a much healthier one once I realized just how beautiful and necessary a spiritually centered life is. The core of my story covers four main areas throughout this book. There are intentionally not specific chapters or sections dedicated exclusively to each of the four areas since it is the integration and application of these areas that are discussed throughout.

1. *Each of us is a spiritual being that has been created to coexist with a divine wisdom.*

2. *Within everyone's spirit exists a communication of divine guidance that is based on the power of unconditional love.*

3. *A universal language exists between our spirit and all other sources of spiritual energy.*

4. *The evolution of each person's spirit is solely dependent upon each individual's sincere, willful effort to "be more of God."*

Throughout this book, I will do my best to inspire you with a different perspective regarding who you are. I encourage you to make notes in the margins, highlight certain sections, jot down questions, or keep a journal of your thoughts to make this book your own. While universal wisdom can certainly be communicated in a simple yet profound manner, we should each be aware that our capability to fully comprehend this knowledge is strictly dependent upon our own personal level of spiritual development. I remain confident that the words expressed within this book will offer most readers a more enlightened understanding about themselves. That being said, I would encourage you to reread the book, perhaps multiple times if need be, to gradually allow its messages more opportunities to inspire and change you. In addition, allow yourself to compare what you learned the last time you read it to what you know today in the present moment. This will allow you to become more aware of the change and growth that has taken place within your own spirit over time. I promise that those who sincerely seek universal truth will be divinely led to a higher awareness and a more profound perspective of themselves.

I am confident there will be many moments when the words within this book may challenge you to grasp their full meaning. Please do not allow your mental doubt to make you suspicious about whether this book is really a source of insight and inspiration to grow from. Many times over the past eleven years, my mental doubt, disbelief, and faithlessness hindered my spiritual progression. I felt abandoned and alone at those moments and longed for helpful support and guidance to reduce my confusion. Never let your mental skepticism dissuade you from committing to your own spiritual growth. Your mental fears, your disbeliefs, and their skepticism of your spirit were purposely created by God to challenge your spirit by testing your spirit's blind faith to make only love-based choices. Only you and you alone are capable of seeing and knowing the real truth about yourself.

If we want the journey of discovering who we are and what the real purpose of life is to be a powerful and revealing one, we need to put forth a sincere, willful effort and nothing less. I honestly hope those readers with a vested interest in aligning their lives with a more profound existence find most of the answers they seek in this book. I also hope this book can be a continual source of help, encouragement, and inspiration in the quest to "be more of God."

As I often tell the audiences of my spiritual classes, events, and workshops, I am not interested in trying to convince anyone that all the knowledge I am about to present is the absolute truth. Instead, it is much more important to share my knowledge and insight in a manner that always allows others the freedom to conclude for themselves whether my words are in fact universally truthful.

Acknowledgements

Writing this book was the most challenging endeavor I have ever chosen for myself. The words, concepts, and understanding contained within these pages represent a love-based philosophy born from my effort to live more spiritually centered. During this transformation of self, I became forever grateful to those people who sincerely offered their help, support and encouragement when I most needed it.

I am forever grateful to my wife, Michelle. Overcoming resistance from others, you stayed true to your inner sense of love. Your continued faith, support, reinforcement, compassion, strength, and unwavering love is without equal and my greatest blessing.

To my daughter, Courtney: My responsibility and commitment to be a good, loving father and a source of inspiration that you're proud of influenced my change. The strength I summon to commit myself to fulfilling this change represents how much *I love you*.

Thank you, Jim, for being open to the truth, listening to your spirit, and empowering me with your faith. And, for patiently holding my hand while reassuring me with your smile. Maybe you can pay for lunch once in a while!

Yanni. Thank you for your friendship, your companionship, and being a great source of insight. I truly understand why Jaime saw you as a Greek god!

To Siobhan H.; Michelle G.; Susan A.; Denise A.; Barbara P.; Susan U.; Holly D.; Cindy R.; Michelle and Vince; Donna A.; Tim and Marissa; Laura K.; Leigh P.; Ellen H.; Joanne K.; Sharon S.; and Marnie K.: thank you for your helping hands in creating opportunities for my events, services, and galleries to reach the lives of others.

I am grateful to Alyssa, Maryann, and Kathleen, whose editing skills turned my often esoteric words into a more digestible and desirable form of reading.

God, thank you for helping me see the truth.

PART ONE

Being "More of God"

CHAPTER 1

A Little Background

Our contributions to those we love are most valuable once we've grown capable of providing the guidance, love, and wisdom needed to build a happy and rewarding life.

I grew up in a very strict Catholic household in Hamilton, New Jersey. My parents placed me in after-school religion classes until I was twelve while making sure we attended church almost every Sunday. My religion taught me to pray to God if I needed God's assistance or guidance; hence, my prayers usually centered on requests for some sort of divine intervention to improve my life and make it less difficult to endure.

After passing several physical, mental, and academic tests, at the age of twenty-two, I completed four months at a very committed and intense police academy that fulfilled my requirements to be a patrol officer for the Hamilton Township Police Department. For the next twenty-seven years of my life, I worked as both an undercover narcotics and a criminal investigations detective. In general, I was extremely proud of what I accomplished professionally. Apart from primarily conducting investigations involving drug-related offenses, homicide, and other violent crimes, I was an affiant in over 120 search-warrant affidavits, including a multi-jurisdictional and multi-state wiretap investigation into methamphetamine distribution. One investigation I worked on involved an armed robbery case in which my actions introduced brand-new New Jersey criminal case law. After my actions in this investigation were ruled lawful by a Superior Court judge, all police officers in New Jersey held more authority to pursue visual evidence of a crime on private property without first obtaining a search warrant.

I was in my mid-forties when my life basically fell apart. For one thing, I separated from and eventually divorced my wife, Michelle, to whom I'd been married for sixteen years. Leaving her also meant separating from my twelve-year-old daughter, Courtney, and moving from a wonderful home I co-owned with Michelle to renting the first floor of a two-story home. Not wishing to affect the lifestyle my daughter grew up with, I started from scratch and soon found myself tens of thousands of dollars in debt. Depression, loneliness, and anxiety were my constant companions.

Fatherhood was a role I took very seriously, no matter what I might have been experiencing on a personal level. I made sure to maintain the best relationship I could manage with my daughter. Being able to guide Courtney and help her achieve a life much greater than my own was a personal goal for me that had no equal. In hindsight, the single most important thing that motivated me to become "more of God" was my desire to be the kind of father Courtney would be truly proud of.

CHAPTER 2

My Poor Personal Philosophy

People should not be viewed as our main source of love.

The sort of insight and knowledge I received from my family, from school, and from society growing up did not provide me with the wisdom to make my adult life happier and better. For many years I struggled, trying desperately to earn success, love, and happiness through money, power, or other people. When life failed to yield the sort of results I expected or wanted for myself, I searched for excuses to blame others. I also became rather angry whenever I failed to receive the level of emotional support I wanted and desired. Most of my relationships ended with disappointment because I refused to view myself in a truthful way and subject myself to truthful change. What I hadn't understood at the time was that the so-called philosophy I was taught about love and relationships—one that taught me how to inflict guilt; exercise control; wrongly influence; and manipulate other people to be a dedicated source of love for me—was a poor one that would inevitably always fail.

My deception and manipulation included intentionally aligning my words, actions, and personal opinions with others to encourage or strengthen their attraction toward me. Obtaining someone's acceptance and approval made me feel loved and appreciated, if only for a brief time. I learned at an early age that most people don't want to hear the truth and that one should avoid addressing it directly, especially in public. But again, applying such a "philosophy" to my life proved faulty; for it prevented me from developing the necessary courage to express myself truthfully with people I wished to have a more meaningful relationship with. Later on, when I finally took an honest appraisal of myself, I realized that when I buried the truth and deprived myself of my own true voice, I was preventing myself from becoming someone I could be proud of. More importantly, I wasn't fulfilling any real purpose for myself.

I also came to the realization that most of the people I was choosing to gain acceptance, recognition, and help from were incapable of demonstrating a loving and wise way to live their own lives, let alone possessing the real wisdom and love to add to my own. This made me aware that when I sought help and guidance from those unwise and unloving people, I unknowingly allowed their "unproven knowledge" to influence my actions, my choices, and my own potential as well.

CHAPTER 3

The Two Sources of Knowledge Within

To fully comprehend the higher meaning of our human experiences we must start with the right perspective of ourselves.

Initially, I was essentially clueless about how to find a direct path to a higher wisdom. I also wondered if it were even possible. My vision of God at that time equated to an unreachable, profound being that communicated absolute truth and was filled with unconditional love. So, to start with, I tested my perceived vision of God by applying it to my own life. If God is always truthful, I thought, then perhaps I should try being truthful about myself.

I decided to spend at least several weeks reviewing my own past in depth as truthfully as possible, just to see if anything useful surfaced. I revisited both positive and negative experiences from childhood to the present day, but I mainly made a marked effort to learn more about what influences I was affected by that caused me to make choices that hadn't resulted in positive and loving outcomes (choices either I had made myself or that others had advised me to make). Many of these events I longed to be able to go back and do differently now, causing me deep regret of a sort I had never quite experienced previously. Viewing these unloving, negative past events of my life in a truthful way allowed me to see clearly my part in causing them and how I could have stopped them from happening at all. I'd never realized how challenging it would be to look at myself so honestly while accepting a true conclusion of how unwise my personal philosophy of life had been all those years. I can still attest that it was the most humbling experience I have ever had. At the same time, speaking the truth about myself to myself had an innate power to it that sprouted a sense of freedom within me. It was as if I became free from some inner burden to speak the truth.

As I'd mentioned, I was incorrectly taught early in life that being truthful would not just create problems in my relationships with others; it would also prevent me from manifesting the positive outcomes I personally wanted for my life. Yet by great contrast, the experience of truthfully examining my past to learn more about myself had certainly been positive and uplifting. I now understand how this simple but courageous effort truly kick-started my transitional and powerful transformation of self.

During my life review, several moments seemed to capture my attention and interest over and over. By thoroughly examining these moments, I became aware that all my past choices were influenced by not one but two different sources of knowledge, both of which existed within me. What was interesting to me was that each source had the ability to affect my decision-making directly. The first source was using the thinking process of my brain to ascertain the truth. In a convincing way, my thinking would favor a specific set of reasons or way of reasoning that it assumed would satisfy whatever I wanted a truthful answer about. The second source seemed to be some inner ability to know knowledge that answered any sincere need I had before I had a chance to think about it. When I received information from the second source, it always resonated from within the center of my body, from around my heart. This was quite unlike receiving information from the first source—in that case, the information resonated from the middle of my head. Oddly, it was as if I had two different "points of view" or "centers of perspective" from which to draw information and guidance. I felt compelled to know more about these two sources of knowledge, including whether their guidance had a different effect on my life or if they were on par with each other. As I spent more and more time contemplating this, I paid close attention to the kind of knowledge each source possessed and how each source guided me to that knowledge. I noticed that the information from the second source came very quickly yet subtly, much like a confident, spontaneous whisper. For instance, I recalled moments in the past when I subtly knew or could sense that the words I was about to speak weren't loving, but I still spoke them anyway; and I knew or could sense that the choice I was about to make to expose myself to certain situations and people had a good chance of resulting in a negative or series of negative experiences, but I still chose it. Sometimes this "confident, spontaneous whisper of knowledge" lingered within me for an extended period of time after I chose not to follow it, as if it was trying to remind me of what I should have done.

The more I studied this inward communication, the more it became clear that the message I was supposed to get from it involved the importance of self-love, even though at the time I wasn't quite sure what love actually was. In fact, I was extremely unprepared to under-stand or appreciate what God's "higher purpose" for creating love was. Most of us support the notion of having love in our lives, yet how many of us have actually had a conversation about how love works or can provide a universal explanation for it?

I became keenly aware of a consistent effort from the thinking process of my brain to purposely resist or dismiss any information coming from my second source of knowledge. For instance, if I had a spontaneous inner sense to be openly honest with a friend about a change it was apparent he needed to make in his life, one he was purposely avoiding, I usually noticed that immediately after receiving the inner sense to speak up, my thinking brain would immediately come up with a list of reasons or reasoning to persuade me why doing so would not result in a very positive outcome. My thinking brain seemed to contradict the spontaneous inner sense of guidance I first received.

As a result of this insight, I then asked myself which part of me first received the sudden inner guidance to speak the truth and whom my thinking brain was speaking to when it offered its rebuttal. After much contemplation, I came up with even more questions, such as: "What if having two different sources of guidance to freely choose from is connected to my higher purpose? Is my inner knowing a communication of my spirit? If so, is my inner knowing actually my spirit receiving knowledge and only it is capable of receiving God's guidance on its own and not my physical brain?" I then became inspired with another inquiry: "Is it possible that everyone has similar experiences where knowledge is shared with each via his or her spirit? If so, is it possible most people are unaware that our inner knowing is actually our spirit receiving knowledge and guidance because they haven't been properly educated about it? In connection with this same thought, is it also possible that this inner communication comes across as a "whisper" because so far, I haven't placed much faith in it? If I were to place more faith in it, might this inner sense of knowledge and guidance emerge into a much stronger one—one that the thinking process of my brain no longer had the strength to dismiss or ignore?"

Most people, I was sure, would agree on some level or another that at least a portion of who they are consists of a spirit. Even in Christianity and Catholicism, the word spirit is frequently used. Yet ironically, I cannot recall even a single instance of being taught how to experience proof of the living spirit within me. What I did see proof of growing up was how my thinking brain did a very poor job at providing me with the necessary wisdom to enrich and educate my life. This led me to believe that perhaps receiving higher wisdom was not something my brain was divinely created to do on its own. I began to accept the possibility that God purposely created our physical brain incapable of sincerely knowing, on its own, the difference between truth and non-truth. I began to have a clearer understanding of how deceptive my thinking brain's guidance could be whenever I used it as my main source of wisdom. It was beginning to make sense that if I were searching for a way to receive profound spiritual guidance, it might be necessary to develop and use my own spirit to do so.

CHAPTER 4

"Knowing Knowledge"

Blind faith is a test of our spirit's will to overcome any adversity that challenges our inner guidance, without first knowing the outcome of that guidance.

I was now feeling or sensing a strong "inner need" for a deeper explanation of the guidance and knowledge that was being communicated from within. To start, I first sought to understand what this strong "inner need" was and where it actually originated from. To me, what I had a strong "inner need" to do was an honest form of guidance that compelled me toward a very specific direction with a specific purpose. But where did this "inner need" to do something come from? Did I create it on my own, or did it come from some external intelligent source, like God? For the moment, I decided to view the source of my inner guidance as a kind of personal companion who was trying to give me and my life a helpful push forward.

Receiving inner knowledge or guidance that I somehow knew was the truth always felt more inspirational than anything else. At the same time, I never sensed that I was being forced to accept it as the truth or to follow its guidance. Instead, I felt I had a choice about accepting and listening to what the knowledge was guiding me to do, meaning I was free to place faith in it or not. In this moment, I wasn't quite sure why, but

I felt that having this freedom was an important part of understanding the origin of this inner guidance.

At this point, I began to entertain a strong belief that I was a spiritual being, divinely created and with a natural ability to receive information that was not only truthful but designed to lead me toward self-discovery, self-help and self-healing. Simultaneously, I began to view the thinking process of my brain as a separate source of knowledge, and because it was presently a more dominant source, it could easily cause me to doubt and thus resist the potential of my own spirit. If this was all hypothetically true, I wondered if there was a way for my spirit to be the dominant source instead. If so, would that significantly increase the amount of inner knowledge, guidance, and potential wisdom I could receive to resurrect my life?

I was very unclear about how to tell the difference between knowledge that came from my thinking brain and knowledge received through my spirit, so I began to carry a notebook everywhere and take detailed notes about experiencing both types. One of the differences I often encountered was that my inner knowing would always reach my awareness more quickly than my thinking. In addition, I noticed that whenever my spirit received knowledge or guidance, it was always helpful but dependent upon my faith in it. I had to have and show faith in what my spirit received by taking corresponding action or verbalizing what was communicated. It's one thing to meditate or pray in solitude, which can be beneficial; however, I aimed to apply and take action based upon what my spirit received as a way of demonstrating faith in growing my spirit and in helping others.

I eventually concluded that there were four different "tests" I could conduct to find out whether the information I'd received came from my spirit as opposed to my brain. If I could sincerely claim that the knowledge did not come from me but from a source that was outside me, it passed the first test. If the knowledge resonated within my body's center (heart) as opposed to my head's center (brain), it passed the second test. If I felt the knowledge or guidance came to me in a very quick, inspirational way, the third test was passed. To pass the fourth test, the knowledge or guidance communicated had to serve a loving purpose for myself or others. Lastly, any knowledge that passed the above tests and was followed by my brain attempting to dismiss or doubt that knowledge's credibility to be the truth further supported this hypothesis that the information had come through my spirit and not my thinking brain.

CHAPTER 5

Understanding How Not to Think

Our only true possession is the "amount of God" we become during our physical lifetime.

At this point in my spiritual exploration, I was beginning to release the old identity of myself and form a more godly perspective about who I was. I was now supporting the belief that I was an intelligent source of spiritual energy created with a divine purpose to "be more of God." My physical body and physical brain were created to assist my spirit in this evolution. When I looked at the bigger picture of these possibilities, it made sense that if my spirit had existed since my birth, perhaps it was nothing more than a lack of so-called spiritual education that had prevented my spirit's communication from expanding. If so, what might life be like if we all experienced an education about our spirit at an early age while being taught how to use wisely our physical lifetime to fulfill our divine purpose to be more of God? (Not just any God, by the way, but a divine intelligence who had created a universal way of life solely based on the communication and power of unconditional love.)

I'd finally found the beginning I'd been searching for, one that offered the hope I'd been craving. I committed myself to a new way of experiencing my life through developing the "inner knowing" of my spirit and allowing it to be my main source of guidance and insight. To accomplish this, my approach was to avoid using the thinking process of my brain as the primary means for interpreting my life. Yet when I made this choice, I didn't remotely comprehend how significant the effort would be. Actually, how much of a *lifetime* effort it would be.

First, I had to ascertain whether I was even capable of functioning without thinking about what I was about to do at any given moment or any future one. I began by placing myself in a comfortable position on my couch to see if I could focus my attention on becoming aware of my own thinking process. Within a short time, I found that I did indeed possess a natural ability to recognize information that hailed directly from my thinking brain. Throughout each day, I acknowledged any information that came from my thinking brain and labeled it as such. The more time I spent improving on this skill, the easier it became for me to know not only when it was happening, but even when it was about to happen. Something else I considered significant then occurred to me. I asked myself, "What part of me, specifically, is demonstrating the ability to become more aware of my thinking? If it's my spirit, could I now be witnessing evidence of who I really am?"

Once I reached what I considered to be a credible level of awareness to recognize my thinking, I decided that the next step would be to prove whether I was capable of preventing myself from thinking, period. I followed the same process of being aware of my thinking while blindly summoning any natural power to compel my thinking to cease. I was hoping to possess a power that could not only minimize, deter, and prevent the thinking process of my brain from controlling and influencing my life but release me from following its inept guidance. Could I potentially suffer less mental anguish, anxiety, and anger if I could prevent my brain from thinking on its own? Is mental confusion what I end up with when I turn to my brain to solve problems it isn't capable of solving or seek answers it is not capable of receiving? And, if this is true, did God purposely design the responses of mental confusion, anger, and torment in everyone's lives to encourage people to search for a better source of help and wisdom?

Initially, I found it a losing battle to maintain any respectable length of time to sustain a state of nonthinking. When I did manage it, within a minute or two, my mental doubt always succeeded in preventing me from expanding the length of time. At this point, I considered my brain a superior adversary and source of resistance to my spirit's growth. I felt frustrated by this. If a universal God of Love truly existed, then why would God create such a problematic relationship between my thinking brain and my spirit? Why wouldn't God instead establish a harmony of existence between them? While I contemplated these questions, I realized I could not attest to one single offering, by my thinking brain of spontaneous, loving support toward the existence, communication, or growth of my own spirit.

Several weeks into this process, I was finally able to maintain a nonthinking "state of existence" for up to thirty minutes, thanks to faith, perseverance, and courage. (I'd begun the process spending several days at each incremental stage—first for more than a minute or so, then for five minutes, then ten, then twenty, and finally thirty minutes.) This milestone—and that's exactly how I experienced it—did not happen even close within the time frame I'd originally planned for myself. Regardless, I remained sincerely committed and faithful to the process each day, over and over again. I refused to support any reasoning that might prevent me from continuing with the progress I was making.

During this process, I experienced several moments where I became suddenly inspired with what I considered "God lessons or life lessons" my spirit needed to demonstrate. I felt strongly that I received these lessons through my spirit because this information came to me while I was in a state of nonthinking while passing the four tests I now had for spirit communication. Although I didn't understand this at the time, during these moments of inspiration I had actively surrendered sole ownership and control over my life.

One inspiring moment helped me to see a correlation regarding previous periods of my life in which I prayed to God for what I per-sonally wanted from God as well as what I personally wanted God to do for me. In both instances, my praying in the past and, later, quieting my thinking to receive higher guidance, I was temporarily surrendering sole ownership and control over my life by making a sincere, willful request for God's help. The main difference between my past methods of praying for God's help and the new method of quieting my thinking to receive God's guidance is that with the latter, I was more learned on how to use my spirit to listen to God's reply. Quieting my thinking brain shifted my spirit to the forefront of my life, thus taking over all responsibility of receiving and interpreting any knowledge or guidance that God might be replying with. The absence of this single most important component kept me from receiving the past answers I had spent years praying for. Is it true that God's specific wisdom and guidance for each of us can only be received through our own spirit? If that is the case, my next step had to be demonstrating my love for this inner guidance by faithfully and blindly following it. Perhaps the divine help I had always been searching for also existed in those many "spontaneous whispers of insight, guidance, and knowledge" that I had mentally dismissed as nonsense.

During one particular sitting to quiet my thinking, I was inspired with the question: "What can I truthfully say is a product of my own creation?" The question led me to a deeper understanding that I should never treat anything I did not personally create on my own as mine. Similarly, I realized, I should never attempt to control that which does not belong to me.

An ideal example of what I mean is nature. Nature is not something I created; therefore, it is not mine to control or change. Rather, I should view it as a "gift" for me to enjoy and learn from; one I am welcome to explore and use, yet with the responsibility that I do so in a loving way. Going one step further, I can validly applied such a theory to human relationships. If nature is a "gift" for people to enjoy in a loving way, can one person be a "gift" to another, as long as two people communicate with each other in loving ways? For example, is the amount of time that two people freely choose to share with each other dependent upon each other's ability to communicate in an unconditionally loving way? In my view of all of this, I could now see how the greatest gift I could offer someone else would be my genuine ability to affect that person's life in a wise and loving way. Simultaneously, the greatest gift I could bestow upon myself would be choosing only genuinely loving and wise people to share my life with.

I was becoming more aware of love as a divine form of communication that never fails to be spiritually helpful in one way or another. God has bestowed on us the amazing gift of personal freedom, which allows us to choose freely whom we wish to be loving toward and spiritually helpful to. By demonstrating how to be helpful and loving to myself first, I am more capable of recognizing such accomplished abilities within others who can behave in kind. This prevents me from being seduced by people who are not demonstrating a way of life based on the foundation of unconditional love but are very adept at presenting themselves as if they are.

The development of this knowledge swiftly altered my previous beliefs that I'd been too slow in my personal growth and development to quiet my thinking brain. What I learned from this insight was to be grateful and thankful for any progress I was making. It wasn't the amount of progress that was truly important—it was the fact that progress was being made in the first place. Seeing progression in my ability to quiet my thinking brain meant that the process I was following was proving itself. This was the evidential proof I had originally asked for and needed to experience.

While maintaining this direction and developing my process, I unconditionally wrote down any insight or knowledge that I received through my spirit or questions that arose. After all, if this knowledge was actually coming from a higher wisdom, then I should be giving it the respect that it very much deserved! The one question that kept prodding me to know more about was the following: "What specific part of me is demonstrating the power to quiet my thinking brain?" In other words, what was the origin of this power that had repeatedly demonstrated a natural ability to be "aware" of my thinking and able to quiet my brain's desire to think on its own? After a couple of weeks of remaining hopeful for an updated answer to this question, I became inspired with the following one: The power that allows me to quiet my thinking brain comes from the will of my spirit. The revelation of this answer proved an extremely enlightening moment. It made sense that if I were demonstrating faith in my spirit, perhaps that faith was nurturing strength into the will of my spirit. And if the will of my spirit was growing stronger, perhaps that added strength was capable of overcoming and quieting my thinking brain.

Unbeknownst to me, the growth of my spiritual will began to slowly shift my spirit back to what I will call its "original position at the forefront of my life." This means that my spirit was once again becoming the more dominant voice in my life after being relegated to the background for so long.

This triggered an ever more expanded perspective of myself. I seemed to possess three separate strengths:

1. *God created my brain with a mental strength.*

2. *My body was created with a physical strength.*

3. *The strength of my spirit became otherwise known (to me) as my spiritual will.*

In retrospect, by unknowingly but faithfully shifting my spirit "back" to the forefront of my life, I subsequently realigned all three of my personal strengths into the order they were divinely meant to exist, which is "Spirit, Mind, Body" as opposed to the more familiar yet unnatural alignment of "Brain, Body, Spirit." This natural alignment enables me to be more spiritually centered and places the evolution of my spirit as my most important purpose or priority. I could now see how an unnatural alignment of the three had made me more brain-centered and had caused me to pursue a path where I only received what my brain mentally wanted for itself. (Note: Later, I explain the difference between a thinking brain and a cooperative visual mind.) Demonstrating and maintaining a natural alignment of "Spirit, Mind, Body" had the potential to lead to a major spiritual transformation that could hold the key to increased self-awareness and enlightenment.

CHAPTER 6

My Changing Perspective of Myself

By allowing our choices to naturally unfold we get a glimpse of how wise we actually are.

As I continued to pursue what I viewed as the "evolution of my spirit," I slowly became more aware of the extreme importance of surrendering sole control and ownership over my life. Learning how to "be more of God" wasn't just about adopting the knowledge I received through my spirit or mentally remembering knowledge I gleaned from a book or received from others. It was about serving by example. What would be the purpose of being inspired with a higher wisdom and perspective if I didn't personally demonstrate the faith and the courage to allow that wisdom to truthfully change me?

The evolution of our spirit is achieved by demonstrating or spiritually carrying out the wisdom we have learned for ourselves during real-life situations and challenges. For instance, when I learned about surrendering sole ownership over my life to reestablish my spiritual coexistence with God, it meant to me that I was only meant to do my part in my life and allow God to do God's part in my life. To put this into practice, I learned to give up making choices on my own, only to choose and act on the knowledge I spiritually sensed was loving for my life and never attempt to control the outcome of those choices. If I were capable of accomplishing this, I would be allowing my life to unfold naturally, according to God's will.

CHAPTER 7

Being More Spiritually Centered

Our human existence holds an endless series of opportunities divinely designed to spiritually educate us on how to create a more loving life for ourselves.

I continued to improve my ability to quiet the thinking process of my brain, and I was able to do so for much longer periods of time. Following this process seemed to give my spirit the strength it needed to remain at the forefront of my life. I was discovering that God purposely created faith with a divine power to nurture personal growth. Now it was up to me to use its power to nurture strength and growth into my spiritual will. In the past, I had foolishly created an imbalance within myself when I placed more faith in my mental interpretation of my experiences rather than my spirit's interpretation of my experiences. Now I realized that my real goal in life is not to reach a point of mental self-satisfaction but to strengthen the will of my spirit to satisfy the higher will of God.

It wasn't until about four or five months after moving into my new apartment and being completely on my own that I first developed the ability to continually sense a loving spiritual presence within myself. While I wasn't receiving the kind of inner guidance and knowledge in the godlike way I would have wished and hoped for, I was receiving a greater quantity of knowledge through my spirit that began to expand into words, visions, and images that I had to properly interpret the meaning of to fully understand the insight I was being given. Every single detail and aspect of the words, visions, and images I received had a great story to tell.

Now more than ever, whenever I quieted the thinking process of my brain, I became abundantly aware of a very strong sense of inner peace emerging from within me. It was similar to entering into a comfortable, loving home after being away from it for a long period of time. It wasn't something I intentionally asked to receive. It was more like a natural response to successfully reducing or quieting my thinking. I viewed this inner peace as a meaningful response purposely created by God to help me understand that this is the path I needed to follow to move my life forward.

The evolution of my own spirit to be more of God was indeed an independent journey. Within this journey of self, it made sense to me that if a universal, loving God truly existed, God would provide the same opportunity for guidance and help for everyone. If it were true that God created my spirit with a divine purpose to be more of God, and if my spirit had to learn how to do that on its own, it made sense that God created specific responses to encourage me toward a specific way to fulfill that purpose. I remember thinking around this time how amazing it would be to have a universal understanding that explained how our perceived experiences of anger, happiness, confusion, peace, worry, and fear were actually personal responses created by God to educate us about the difference between living a more spiritually centered loving life and living a life with a lack of self-love for it.

Without fail, each and every time I quieted the thinking process of my brain, a growing state of peace resounded within me. Around this time, the majority of the insight that was coming to me suggested that my spirit's growth and the growth of my life were directly linked to the communication of unconditional love. Through this insight, I slowly grew to understand how my greatest challenge wasn't just recognizing the loving choice to make—it was demonstrating the will and strength to always make that loving choice. A good demonstration of this is when I summoned the courage and will to calmly speak the truth in a loving way during a moment of personal adversity.

CHAPTER 8

On Surrendering to My Spirit and Being Spiritually Learned

Wisdom is universal truth that explains a way of life solely based on the communication and power of unconditional love that equally affects us all.

I hoped that spiritually willing myself into a deeper sense of peace while steadily increasing the length of time I could maintain such a peaceful state would guide me toward a more spiritually centered existence. It was now clear that if I resisted relinquishing sole control over my life, I would interfere with my ability to accept and receive higher wisdom *and* accept sincere help from others. Practicing this life lesson did not mean I was to accept help blindly from just anyone. Instead, I needed to place blind faith in my own potential and ability to recognize the people and opportunities that would only add to my life and not subtract from it.

All people were created to be spiritually equal but not equally spiritual. The only real difference between people is the amount of wisdom and love their spirit possesses. The difference between the way we physically appear to one another is meaningless. Physical appearance does not unite people; only love does. When we base our lives on the higher wisdom our spirit possesses, we are spiritually centered and spiritually learned. Those who do not pursue a spiritually centered existence are spiritually unlearned. Understanding this difference made it possible for me to avoid judging people as being either good or bad. I came to the realization that our human existence is an educational and evolutionary process that everyone's spirit is going through, which is why I now view myself and others as either spiritually learned or spiritually unlearned.

Viewing people as either spiritually learned or spiritually unlearned seemed to convey a much more loving viewpoint of myself and others. The power of love is always helpful to our spirit, our lives, and our overall happiness. To be loving toward myself, I had to focus on how to be helpful to my spirit's growth, which in turn gave me a response of happiness. The same was true about other people. If I wished to be loving toward other people, I had to learn how to use my words and actions in a way that was helpful in the education of their spirit, which in turn would make me happy. Love is an experience and a power that we sense and feel. It is an experience that has no equal. Learning to surrender my life to a higher wisdom was allowing me to experience a more loving existence while making me feel much happier about myself.

CHAPTER 9

Attaining a State of Spiritual Oneness

Spiritual Freedom is experienced when our ability to pursue what we sense a natural love for is not compromised by outside forces.

I continued to be open to and grateful for any knowledge received through my spirit. I did not question the amount of inspirational guidance I received or spiritual improvement that took place; I was simply grateful it was finding its way into my life. As I continued to pursue making my spirit my primary source of wisdom, I began to experience an even deeper sense of spiritual peace that eventually grew into a spiritual state of quietness.

A spiritual state of quietness is attained when we remain so focused on receiving inner knowledge and wisdom that we become disconnected from any outer distractions delivered via our five senses. It was amazing to me knowing I had an ability that could disconnect me from and prevent outside nonmeaningful noise and distractions from influencing me. This ability proved to me how strong my spiritual will was becoming and what it was capable of. I wanted to strengthen it even further, so sometimes I would sit in front of a radio or television, crank the volume up high, and remain intent upon staying spiritually centered. After attaining a state of spiritual quietness, I hung on to see if there was something more. There was: after a little experimenting, I learned how to achieve a state of spiritual stillness, which I attained by focusing my spiritual will on wholly existing within the moment while disconnecting from any noise and the world around me. Living in the moment contributes greatly to reaching a state of spiritual stillness. It was this state specifically that made me feel as if I had just reentered the natural state of existence from which my spirit and all spirits are created. From this place, the knowledge I received had a direct correlation with whatever I made myself aware of and really seemed to flow, meaning I had reached a state of spiritual centeredness where an increased flow of inner knowledge occurred because my spirit had attained more of its natural state of existence. In this natural state of existence without other worldly distractions, it, my spirit, was now much more capable of participating in the type of conversations it was divinely created to have.

It is this combination of being spiritually still while expanding awareness to all one is part of that helps a person achieve a state of spiritual oneness. Upon reaching this state of existence, the person you know as "you" becomes vague and undefined. You learn that you are more than you originally thought and have a greater sense of whole than you ever anticipated. In essence, you can spiritually sense a much closer bond and relationship with God. You begin your journey of distancing yourself from any particular human identity and identify more with your spiritual self. At the same time, the knowledge your spirit can receive quickens while becoming more abundant in detail. It is hard to explain, but time becomes one big moment. As a result, your life pace slows down to represent living in that moment.

PART TWO

My Personal Experiences

CHAPTER 10

The Author of Authors

The communication of love is divinely guided to always be spiritually helpful.

As I continued to pursue longer and longer periods of time holding onto a state of spiritual oneness, whatever I focused my spiritual awareness on resulted in a return of higher comprehension and insight regarding how I and every aspect of my life are all linked to God and the power of unconditional love. The comprehension of the knowledge and insight I was now receiving about my spirit's evolution to be more of God was a challenge but never too profound for me to understand, and it was always delivered to me in a very gradual way and in a digestible amount. It is important to note that I never felt as if any of this higher knowledge was being forced upon me, nor did I ever sense God wanted something in return for sharing this heightened understanding with me. To me, being helpful to someone without wanting anything in return for that help was a demonstration of communicating in an unconditionally loving way—which is exactly what I felt God was demonstrating to me. Becoming aware of how wisdom and knowledge was reaching my spirit gave me the insight of how to improve my own ability to communicate with others in a much more meaningful way.

While I'd never really read literature that involved God, angels, spirits, spiritual intuition, or spiritual growth, I now found myself experiencing a "strong need" for such material, spending upward of $200 at the local bookstore. Even though I was currently many thousands of dollars in debt, if I was going to commit to this new way of life, I was going to do it full throttle! After all, if the communication I was receiving was truly from a source of God, I had to have complete faith in that God. I didn't realize it at the time, but my "full-throttle" choice was proof of how unconditional my faith actually was. Practicing unconditional, blind faith was a tremendous life lesson for me, primarily because it required me to act on my inner guidance without first understanding why or preoccupying myself with what the outcome might be.

In the past, being "successful" for me meant making the so-called right choices that contributed to my getting what I mentally wanted for myself. On a deeper level, I could now see how success on multiple levels can be achieved when I make the choices my spirit is telling me are right for my life. Meaning, satisfying my spirit's desire to make choices will lead to loving experiences and positive outcomes that my life will prosper from spiritually, socially, and financially. In the beginning of this journey, there were many times when I struggled to know or pinpoint the right or loving choice to make. From those moments, I found that if I simply, via the process of elimination, "crossed out" what I spiritually sensed wasn't right or loving, I would be left with what was. My spiritual sense was my spirit's ability to sense energy that possessed different levels of love, knowledge, and universal truth. Everyone has this spiritual ability, and it is often referred to as common sense— meaning the spiritual ability to sense loving and helpful or unloving and unhelpful energy is common within everyone. Whomever or whatever I spiritually sensed a love for had the strong potential of being helpful to my spiritual growth. When we ask for higher wisdom to help us satisfy our spiritual needs, it may come through non-ordinary and unique experiences that we must demonstrate faith in. The path I needed to follow was not one I would mentally choose. My challenge came from giving up trying to mentally control which path I wanted to take to reach the results and answers I sought.

To improve my ability of better recognizing the energy that indicated what choice was loving and right for my life, each day, I would sit beside the new pile of inspirational books I just purchased. While quietly sitting in front of them, I would choose one at random, and wait for some spiritual sense of whether I should read it. If I was compelled by a spiritual sense to read the book, for me, this inner guidance was suggesting that I would find words that were currently helpful or meaningful to me. Interestingly, this approach often caused me to sense a book was the "right" one, but after reading to the third or fourth page I would suddenly sense a need to put the book down. I became very perplexed about this experience. If I'd initially felt it was the right book to read, why was I suddenly being influenced to put it aside? Then, a sudden thought occurred to me, that maybe it wasn't the book itself that represented the "wrong" choice—perhaps it was how I had gone about reading it. It's of course customary to read a book from beginning to end, the way any author would intend for us to do. However, I was following a "divine author" instead—one who may have been guiding me to read only certain portions of a particular book because only those pages contained the information I needed for either inspiration or contemplation. Being faithful to this sudden thought, I now found myself turning and stopping at certain pages that, after I'd read them, would end up providing me with information relevant to my current life without fail. I no longer spent time reading pages and taking in information I didn't need at the moment. This process taught me that it wasn't how a book's author wished to explain his or her story that was important to me. What was important was following how God wished me to use a book to explain God's story about myself and my life to me.

I took a moment to apply this lesson to my life in a bigger context. Due to my prior lack of faith in my spirit, how often had my thinking brain led me to experiences that weren't necessary or helpful? How many prior "pages" in my life contained unloving experiences merely because I hadn't understood I possessed an innate ability to choose only loving experiences to learn from? All this helped me realize that by designating my spirit as my primary source of wisdom, the "pages" of my life are guaranteed to be abundant with more positive and helpful experiences than in my past. God gave all people the ability to choose what type of life they wish to experience and receive their education from.

I found that the unloving or negative life experiences I had in the past often repeated themselves whenever I lacked the wisdom to prevent them from happening again. I looked at these unloving experiences as my failed life lessons. It is important to take an active role to learn our valuable life lessons, mostly about the influence and power of love, from our personal experiences. The development of my spirit's natural ability to understand the difference between loving and unloving energy is essential. However, the process to develop this ability can be accomplished with very simple exercises, such as choosing the right book to read and how that book is meant to be read, that produce a profound impact. My next step was integrating this ability into my life by making it my new higher standard to determine whom I will openly share my life with and what I will include in my life.

Spoken or written words of people should never be blindly accepted as the truth. People will always use words that represent their current level of wisdom without ever being all wise. God created our spirit with the ability of not only sensing what is and what is not loving but using that sense to build a personal philosophy about a power of love that is universally truthful. It was important to the growth of my spirit that I faithfully allow it to decide what knowledge would support a real philosophy that I could use to enrich my life. So, I decided to use solely this God-created ability to either validate, change, or refute anyone else's words, insights, and ideas that didn't support universal truth. Spiritually filtering (or challenging) all knowledge spoken or written by people not only demonstrated faith in my own spirit—it also encouraged and strengthened trust in my voice before others.

Our discoveries are nothing more than acquiring a deeper and real understanding of something that God had created and already had existed. For me, the existence of a way of life that is based on the energy and power of love was something I was hoping to discover a real and much deeper understanding about.

CHAPTER 11

My Personal Epiphany

Reestablishing our spirit's natural co-existence with higher wisdom is a necessary step in our spirit's evolution.

After several weeks of continually using the inspirational books to develop my ability to sense the energy of love, a wonderful and unexpected moment occurred that can be best described as a literal, personal epiphany. It reshaped the foundation of how I viewed myself and the world around me.

I was holding a book in my hand one evening and waiting to receive a loving sense of what page to choose. I waited several minutes, but the guidance I usually received was missing in action. I began to sense something different about this moment, something significant about not needing to open the book. I surrendered myself to it and was suddenly enlightened with an understanding that completely overwhelmed and enveloped me. My enlightened sense told me that my spirit had the capability not only to know what God knew but to be aware of whatever God was capable of being aware of as well as receiving God's educational viewpoint of all my human experiences. In a nutshell, this is not intended to convey that I was placing myself on a pedestal, but rather, I sensed my co-partnership with God had reached a much stronger and more unified existence.

We are not intended to be kept at a great unreachable distance, as I had been previously taught.

This simple moment of higher awareness changed and enhanced the way I could more completely comprehend the sudden inspirational images, visions, and thoughts my spirit received. This higher awareness I was now more part of steadily grew into a constant flow of knowledge that offered me a deeper education and comprehension of how the power of unconditional love or lack thereof was solely responsible for the positive or negative outcome of everyone's personal choices. If God really created a divine power that influences and affects the lives of all people equally, then I was now receiving my education about this divine communication. In addition, I slowly realized a growing ability that allowed me to receive information and knowledge regarding locations, people, events, and situations that may have occurred in the past that didn't require my physical presence—as well as those current or future. Reflecting on this moment later on, I realized that several things seemed to happen simultaneously:

1. *I experienced an enlightened awareness of God that helped my spirit and my brain to work more cohesively in harmony with each other, which I viewed as a "cooperating visual mind."*

2. *My faith to increase my ability to more completely surrender sole ownership over my life reached a turning point where my spirit's co-partnership with God was now much more entwined and stronger.*

3. *I now held onto an unchallengeable perspective that I am a child of God and God's student first and foremost. My experiences and my life are a giant classroom that possesses and demonstrates universal knowledge for me to study, and to learn and evolve from. And, this universal knowledge is based on how the communication of unconditional love affects everyone's life in an equal way.*

4. *A state of happiness and peace became my core essence, I no longer sensed and felt I was alone, and whatever I personally experienced became much simpler to comprehend.*

5. *My ability to receive information and knowledge from other sources of spiritual energy greatly grew, and my capability to properly interpret and decipher the root meaning of knowledge they shared became much easier to comprehend.*

I came to understand that there is a distinct difference between my visionary mind and my thinking brain. My visionary mind consists of a harmonic union between my spirit and a mentally quiet brain. In this union, my spirit receives truth-based knowledge, which it passes on to my mentally quiet brain in the form of inspired thoughts, epiphanies, ideas, words, and visions. The thinking process of my brain was not meant to interpret or recognize absolute truth, communicate with other sources of spiritual energy, or receive higher wisdom all by itself. The thinking process of my brain needs assistance from my spirit to execute the above functions. Without help from my spirit, my thinking brain routinely offered me reasons of assumptions, possibilities, including illusions, of what the truth may be.

Even though it took several months of dedicated daily faith and effort to reach this epiphany, it only took a moment for that epiphany to change me forever. The spiritual evolution that took place within me greatly exceeded the hundreds of dollars' worth of books I purchased. (*Even though money is socially important to us, it is what we choose to spend our money on that best represents what is most valuable to us.*) My personal epiphany was priceless to me. My new clarity of life initiated a state of happiness, love, peace, simplicity, and wisdom that had never existed in my life before. Eventually, I no longer needed to use the books for assistance. My inspirational task to purchase those books and what I was meant to learn from them had been fulfilled.

I have heard it pontificated that our spirit was placed on Earth to have a "human experience." Instead, I believe our spirit was placed on Earth to demonstrate its capability of bringing a more godly experience to a human existence.

CHAPTER 12

Viewing Life through the Eyes of My Spirit

Disappointment is a response we experience whenever we mistakenly expect a loving gesture from an unloving person

---

My epiphany didn't bless me with omnipotent knowledge about life per se; more accurately, it provided me an expanded perspective of the spiritual presence I felt I already represented. I shifted upward from an ability to temporarily contemplate God to full-time contemplation. It began as soon as I woke up and lasted until I went to sleep. It was as if my spiritual will had enough strength to keep me constantly aware of the divine presence and existence within me. Not only did my perception instantly change—so did my personal philosophy—now unconditional love was the main catalyst for every life experience I ever had as well as every potential one.

In the past, many of my accomplishments—whether personal or professional—were often overlooked, unrecognized, and unacknowledged by spiritually unlearned people. Yet by following communication that can only be received through my spirit, I was beginning to understand how my sincere, willful effort to be more of God never goes unrewarded or unrecognized spiritually or within our social structure.

Throughout my life, I'd routinely wanted and expected to receive loving responses from people who didn't understand how to be loving in the first place. Inevitably unable to receive what I wanted from them, I became angry, disappointed, and resentful. Now I realized that simply by viewing people truthfully (recognizing the wisdom and love that they genuinely had to offer as opposed to what I needed and wanted them to be able to offer), I no longer expected to receive what they couldn't give. Now, when I spiritually sensed an unwise or unloving essence within someone, I fully expected the actions and words from him or her to be unwise and unloving. This simple perception change immensely reduced the personal response of anger, disappointment, and resentment I would normally feel whenever people in my life fell short of what I personally wanted or expected from them.

From this, I learned that I was the main cause of my own anger responses. My spiritual ability to sense people who were unwise and unloving became a kind of entertainment for me. For instance, when sitting in the presence of someone, such as a family member or an acquaintance, whom I sensed had held onto a significant unloving and unwise philosophy, I would entertainingly see how long it took before they spoke words that insulted, criticized, or caused pain to someone else. When I expected unloving people to speak unloving words, I no longer responded in anger but with an entertaining smile of compassion and understanding toward them. I could now see how people were divinely created to express the different levels of love and wisdom they have learned for themselves. I no longer took the words spoken by unwise or unloving people in a personal way. This knowledge helped me reorganize and shift my current relationships with people while helping me wisely choose future ones.

When we commit to the evolution of our spirit, we expand its capacity for love, spiritual will, and wisdom, which cannot be undone once they have been attained. Our spirit cannot undo the level of God it has grown, although our physical brain can easily forget the knowledge we have asked it to remember. While my commitment to my spiritual evolution remained very strong, I did not rule out the possibility that during this transformation, my thinking brain still had the ability to counteract my efforts. Thus, there could be an illusion that my spirit was actively developing and evolving when it really wasn't was always something I allowed myself to be aware of and consider. That's why experiencing as much truthful and real-life validation as possible was extremely important to me. The truth cannot be debated.

At this point in time, I didn't necessarily believe I was spiritually seeing life exactly how God created it to be seen. I felt I was only seeing a very small portion of that total perspective, although it was certainly one that was much more enlightening than anything I had ever experienced so far. When I surrendered myself to the understanding that my spirit and God shared a unified existence, I reinstated the necessary balance that made me see I was more of a "spiritual child"—someone who had quite a lot to learn about the spiritual world than anything else. As a spiritual child, I was being lovingly guided to understand the world around me the way my "spiritual parent," God, created it to be seen. Becoming spiritually aware energetically fed me with knowledge that was truly enlightening on all levels. This was very different from the way I used to receive knowledge—based on the information that my physical sight, hearing, and touch fed to my brain.

Being more spiritually centered enables my spirit to reestablish its natural role of being part of a greater whole. A greater whole refers to being part of the living life energy that exists within every spirit created by God. This living life energy is governed by the communication of love, which serves as the power to keep this energy united together with a universal purpose to be more of God. When we surrender sole ownership over our lives, we are actually surrendering ourselves to the main source of this life energy, being God. Currently, there is a lot of resistance we must face if we choose to reunite with this living life energy. Due to this, being more of God is usually a gradual progression rather than an immediate transformation. This transformation of self can be accomplished within our human lifetime as long as we maintain a growing and evolving love for ourselves and a commitment to seek universal truth.

I had sensed that my spiritual development and evolution represented a personal commitment and achievement that would require a sincere, willful effort on my part. If my effort were not sincere and willful, then the outcome of my effort would fall short. Even though I knew my inner voice of God would always be responsible for guiding me spiritually, it was apparent that I must make a consistent, genuine effort to understand and demonstrate how to truthfully surrender myself to God's voice. We can easily fool ourselves, fool others, and be fooled by other people, but we can never fool God into believing we are making a truthful effort on behalf of our own spiritual growth if we sincerely aren't.

As a result of my commitment to remain in-spirit consistently, it wasn't long until I found myself in the midst of multiple challenges to test my personal faith. There were many moments around this time where I felt enormously overwhelmed by the adversarial aspect of my up-and-coming personal challenges. It's funny how I no longer view those past challenges as enormous; in fact, I wouldn't even consider most of them challenging. The change in standard of what causes me to feel spiritually challenged is the type of validation that truly inspires me continuously to seek a higher standard of what a co-partnership with God is really capable of achieving.

CHAPTER 13

A Demonstration of My Faith

To evolve our spirit, we must seek universal wisdom; lovingly verbalize that wisdom; and then demonstrate blind faith in it.

Up until this time, any validation I experienced of demonstrating knowledge connected to a higher guidance came without much interaction with others. The first considerable challenge that further tested my faith took place one night just a few hours before I was due in at the police precinct for an evening shift. I had been at home making dinner when I realized I was missing a few ingredients. I left the apartment, got in my car, and headed in the direction of a nearby supermarket. I originally intended to drive directly to the store I usually frequented; instead, I yielded to an "inner influence," choosing a route that took me right past it. Eventually, I found myself pulling into the parking lot at the police headquarters.

As I approached the department building, I had a strong urge to drive toward the side parking lot. I was on high alert for anything abnormal and potentially connected to the reason I was being influenced to drive to this location. At the side entrance, I noticed Cindy, one of the police department employees. She was standing outside alone, kind of hunched over, and she had her head in her hands. A bit stunned, I drove past her and continued out of the parking lot.

Once again sensing I was being guided to be at this particular place at this particular time, I focused on being aware of any insight about what I was meant to do next, if anything. Since I still needed to buy food, I finally stopped at the local supermarket. While I waited in the checkout line, I noticed a fresh-flower display and grabbed a bouquet without knowing exactly why. My brain immediately intervened. "Why are you buying those flowers?" it inquired. "For whom? You're wasting your money! Are you intending to give them to Cindy? How do you think she's going to respond to your just showing up at the police station with a bunch of flowers for her?" On and on it taunted.

It's wonderful to claim a belief in God and God's universal guidance, but it's another thing altogether to actually demonstrate faith in what you say you believe in, especially during a moment of mental adversity. So far, my spiritual progression had not come from what I simply knew was the truth but instead from demonstrating what I knew I should do.

The spiritual undertaking I have so far described did not generally yield quick or immediate results. Technically speaking, it is a process that requires us to first demonstrate blind faith by surrendering ourselves to the moments we are guided to experience and allowing that guidance to alter or redirect our everyday life. Mental doubt can easily cause people to lose faith in what's being communicated through their own spirit. Personally, I considered my mental thinking to be my spirit's greatest adversary.

After leaving the supermarket, I drove back to the police department and the spot where I'd seen Cindy. I decided I would just be honest with Cindy about my reason for purchasing the flowers. As soon as I pulled into the parking lot, Cindy left the building and proceeded to walk directly in front of my truck. Being at this particular place at this particular time and watching Cindy literally pass in front of my truck provided me with the hope that my offer of support regarding whatever was upsetting her was a wise one. With confidence, I got out of my truck, flowers in hand. At that same instant, another truck pulled up. The man in the passenger seat rolled down his window and glared at Cindy and me. "Cindy, who the hell is this guy giving you flowers?" he growled.

In that moment, I obviously questioned and doubted the guidance that had placed me in such an awkward position. The man in the truck, who ended up being Cindy's husband, was totally privy to seeing a strange man (me) hand his wife a bouquet of wildflowers—and such a scenario did not represent my idea of a moment that my spirit should have guided me to encounter. I immediately apologized to Cindy's husband, did my best to explain myself, and quickly left what could have developed into a much uglier scene.

For the rest of the evening, I reviewed the events that had transpired. This was the very first time that what I had been directly guided to do involved a purposeful interaction with a person who, in essence, was a professional acquaintance. No matter how many times I reexamined the guidance I'd received, I was insistent that it was indeed knowledge being communicated through my spirit. But if that were accurate, then why didn't the event yield a much more loving and positive outcome?

The next morning when I got to work, I found a white envelope, with my name on it, placed in the middle of my desk. At first glance, I figured it was some sort of interoffice mail. I opened the envelope to discover it was a card from Cindy:

> *Thank you so much for the beautiful flowers—I sincerely appreciate them. The reason I had been crying was because I had just received some very bad news about a loved one who might be dying. I became so upset that I had to leave my office, which is when you spotted me outside. Your flowers really brightened my day and gave me hope. I still laugh about my husband pulling up at the same time you were giving them to me! It is nice to know that there are people out there who care enough about others to reach out (even when they only see you now and*

*again when you pass each other in the hallways). Your
thoughtfulness has inspired me to pass your kindness on
to someone else by doing something nice when they least
expect it. Kindness of that sort should be spread around
more often. If everyone did something nice for someone
else like you did for me, what a better world this would be.*

This experience taught me that perhaps living a spiritually centered life means the communication of love not only connects us with loving people but with people who are in need of help and love. We all need help in our lives at one time or another. How wonderful it is to know that during a time of sincere need, without wanting anything in return, our spirit could be guided to offer someone a kind gesture, supportive voice, or helpful hand that encourages them to hope! Sure—merely having hope might not solve all the problems in the world. But maybe it can get us to trust that all problems can indeed be solved.

I'd doubted my inner guidance because the experience I'd had didn't immediately result in a positive outcome—something that I wanted for myself personally. For me, this was a great life lesson about the importance of maintaining faith while I allowed the outcome of my inner guidance to unfold naturally, at the pace God intended. This valuable life lesson more clearly defined my future role in my co-partnership with God.

CHAPTER 14

Understanding My Dichotomy

A *"divine dialogue" exists between our spirit and all other sources of spiritual energy.*

As the will of my spirit grew in strength, so did my ability to disconnect from the outside hindrances and influences that would normally have had a negative effect on my life. I became more confident and self-assured about the inner knowledge I was receiving and actively sought to abandon my spiritually unlearned ways.

As a child, I was taught that God would only touch my life through some special occurrence or rare intervention. I maintained the belief that the voice of God was divinely special—so special, in fact, that most people would consider it a miracle if it were actually heard. Yet what I was now experiencing seemed to contradict many of those prior beliefs. I was considering the strong possibility that I'd been misinformed. What if the manifestation of God's presence and voice in my life could be a constant occurrence? What if God was constantly dedicated and committed to the spirit within all people, just like a loving birth parent would be to his or her child? What if my prayers were only a small part of the process to receive God's help?

I had literally spent years praying for God's help without believing that I was receiving any help from God. But now I knew the opposite was true. God had been answering my prayers but through a communication only my spirit could receive and interpret. I simply was not taught to have faith in this form of communication. Now, I was finally beginning to understand how to properly interpret God's knowledge and answers that were being communicated to my spirit. To receive God's insight and guidance, I had to first stop my thinking brain from interfering with this spiritual process and communication. When the brain is quieted, our spirit works in harmony with that quiet brain to produce a visionary interpretation of any knowledge our spirit receives. Picture a chalkboard completely covered with random writing. Now try to draw a picture over all that random noise; one that you can clearly see. Now erase everything on the chalkboard, and draw a picture that you can clearly see. Our spirit needs a blank canvas to create the visionary picture that accurately represents the knowledge it is receiving. Some label this visionary process between spirit and physical brain as "having a third eye" or call it "the mind's eye." When we surrender sole ownership over our lives, we shift our spirit "back" to the forefront, making it our main source of knowledge. The knowledge traveling through our spirit is now capable of transferring its higher meaning and insight to the welcoming arms of our quiet brain. We have the power to create this perfect platform upon which all higher knowledge can be transformed into mental images, ideas, words, thoughts, and visions that we can more easily study to comprehend their full meaning and enrich our lives. This "divine dialogue" exists within everyone's spirit. This universal language was created by God to allow a truthful conversation and universal understanding to take place between our spirit, God, and all other sources of spiritual energy (both intelligent and non-intelligent). The difference between intelligent and non-intelligent sources of spiritual energy is as follows: Forms of intelligent spiritual energy have the ability to be self-evolving, which means that they can grow and change. For example, people, animals, and plants have the potential to be self-evolving. By contrast, non-intelligent spiritual examples include items of no inherent ability to self-evolve and grow based upon their own power. For example, a coin or piece of jewelry may be handed down as an heirloom from generation to generation and be associated with the energy of its owners, who have spiritually evolved to varying degrees; however, on its own, the heirloom does not become increasingly spiritually evolved.

CHAPTER 15

An Analogy for the Relationship between the "Soul of God" and My Spirit

It is a defining moment when we can express the necessary self-courage to prevent our own lives from being hindered by others.

Over time, I became more and more aware that the visions I was now experiencing on a regular basis would often present themselves as analogies so I could understand the profound understanding contained within them. One of the first analogies I received occurred while I was having a casual conversation with a good friend. During a moment in our conversation, I became spiritually inspired to better understand the difference between my spirit and the soul of God.

When the vision began, I saw what looked like an enlarged view of the outline of my body. Within the outline of my body were thousands of properly fitted, evenly spaced, and uniquely shaped light bulbs. I knew instantly that the outline of my body and everything within it symbolized my spirit and the light bulbs symbolized the potential essence, or "soul of God," that my spirit was capable of receiving. A very small number of the light bulbs gave off a brilliant and powerful source of light while the rest remained unlit, the space around them dark. It was somehow clear to me that the brilliantly lit light bulbs represented the amount of God's soul or essence that my spirit currently possessed; the unlit light bulbs represented the amount of God's soul that would be available to me when I was ready to receive it. This meant that my spirit and the soul of God were two different things. Whenever my spirit demonstrated an ability to be more of God, it would attain more of God's essence or soul, represented by the illumination of an unlit light bulb. As more light bulbs become illuminated, my spirit becomes more and more enlightened with God's essence. The more enlightened my spirit becomes, the more my spirit coexists in a unified manner with God.

The light-bulb vision generally seemed to be communicating that my spirit's earthly purpose was to be more of God and that it was up to me to use my physical lifetime as a spiritual adventure, one on which I needed to demonstrate an enlightened sense of love, goodness, and wisdom in my daily life. As with all visions, I had immense faith that what I was receiving was the truth. I maintained a very humble approach to all the knowledge I was receiving by keeping it to myself unless I sensed a strong need to share it with someone. However, I could sense the growth of a "strong need" to put myself in some sort of situation that would allow others an opportunity to challenge what I was experiencing and the knowledge these experiences inspired me with.

CHAPTER 16

Being Challenged by My Friends

An act of faith can prove or disprove our personal beliefs, guiding us toward universal truth.

To this point, I had been learning and proving just to myself that it was possible to tap into a constant flow of higher knowledge and guidance that only my spirit could receive. With a progressive influence, this higher knowledge was gradually educating me with a philosophy about how love is divine communication and how its power unites and educates all people in an equal way.

Everyone's lives will eventually witness moments of proof regarding whether our core beliefs actually bear the truth. One of the best ways I felt I could prove my receipt of universal knowledge (wisdom) was to allow myself to be scrutinized and debated openly in some aspect. If I were truly able to receive the higher wisdom of a spiritual God, subjecting that wisdom to the intense scrutiny of others would be a great starting point. This insight and knowledge would be universally accepted by everyone who is present. I had learned that universal truth is knowledge that affects everyone's lives in the same way, with equal results and an explanation about God attached. For instance, when we quiet our thinking brain, a natural state of peace results. This result is universally true for everyone in our world. My role was to explain why a loving God created and allowed this to occur, and I had hoped my answer was universally agreed with by everyone present.

There were many people who chose to distance themselves from me as I pursued an uncommon way to live my life. However, the people I always sensed a closeness with were those to whom I had the honor of teaching martial arts for a few years. I was about thirteen years old when I took my first martial arts lesson. My love for the art kept me dedicated for many years. After reaching a fifth-degree black belt, I used the unique style I learned to open a martial arts studio named American Karate Institute with my good friend and fellow black belt, Ron. We spent many years educating others with our style of martial arts, until one day we left our studio and turned it over to our student black belts, Sarah, Melanie, and Ben. There was a bond between them and me after spending many years together dedicated to the same common purpose. So, I chose to contact them, asking to meet with them at the studio where they were then training. All of them accepted. Although I was ready for this challenge, I was equally nervous that the universal knowledge I believed I had been receiving would inevitably crumble under scrutiny. Yet I viewed Sarah, Melanie, and Ben as true friends, ones I could trust to provide me with the honest feedback I so needed and desired. I said nothing specifically about why I was requesting this gathering. I simply asked that they please view what I planned to present with an open mind and to actively search for ways to disagree, debate, and challenge the knowledge I was going to share with them.

I began our conversation by explaining the spiritual shift my life had taken over the past year, describing how I was attempting to live a way of life that was led by my spirit. I took my time, doing as best I could to explain the existence of a universal, loving God; why I felt all people were created spiritually and divinely equal; how love is a universal guidance; and how our spirit has the potential to participate in a universal language of God. I talked about how inadequately the brain interprets our life experiences and how our spirit does a much more effective job. I detailed the process for shifting my spirit to the forefront of my life and gave my friends insight about what it means to thrive in the natural alignment of "Spirit, Mind, Body" as opposed to the unnatural alignment of "Brain, Body, Spirit." I provided a detailed explanation about how and why God gave everyone "free will," as well as why God granted all of us freedom to choose for ourselves. Finally, I shared with the group my insights about how we are all affected by the communication of unconditional love, which has divine power and hence the ability to guide us throughout life.

Whenever words that communicate a genuine higher wisdom are delivered, our spirit absorbs them like a sponge. When we're in the process of receiving that wisdom, we tend to have a blank, far-off look in our eyes, similar to how someone who's daydreaming appears. While I spoke, I noticed my three friends getting that exact look on their faces, which I honestly enjoyed seeing. Real words of higher wisdom possess such a power that they can put us in a trance-like state of spiritual peace and stillness all on their own. It was truly amazing to witness that far-off stare spread across the faces of everyone present. That being said, I was slightly concerned I might be seeing expressions of boredom on my friends' faces instead! Yet I believed that if my words were capable of capturing the essence of God's wisdom, they would rightfully capture any spirit's undivided attention while simultaneously quieting the thinking brain.

When I finished, I looked around the room and waited for a response. It wasn't until I noticed the clock on the wall that I realized how long I had been speaking. I brought this "time lapse" experience to the attention of the group, and they, too, were amazed by how much time had passed without their realizing it. When our brain is quiet, we are not using it to keep mental track of our time, and therefore it is not immediately aware of how much has passed. I viewed this as another sure indication that my words had indeed conveyed a universal truth.

I strongly encouraged everyone to debate the knowledge I had just shared, but no matter how much they tried (Melanie actually tried for several days afterward), the knowledge I'd shared that evening was accepted and agreed to as being universally truthful for everyone.

Having my knowledge prove itself worthy of intelligent debate provided me with real additional validation as my life was unfolding in a much more spiritual and fulfilling way.

As a result of this informal gathering, Sarah, Melanie, and Ben requested to meet regularly with me to further discuss how to live a more spiritually centered existence. Our meetings continued for many months afterward, and during those months I had the privilege to witness everyone in the group undergo his or her own transformation and evolution. This was another great validation for me. It was amazing to watch how each person took on a more spiritually centered perspective of life, and it was wonderful to witness the new voices, choices, and actions my friends committed themselves to as well. I knew there would be ever more loving and positive experiences for them to enjoy as a result.

Afterward, I became more and more aware of how often I would seem to drift off into a constant stare. To me, this was a positive sign that I was learning to maintain a spiritual state of centeredness and inspiration during my everyday tasks. I was getting better at disconnecting and removing myself from the worldly noise around me while increasing my focus on the communication between my spirit and other sources of spiritual energy, such as God's wisdom. I felt that the strength of my spiritual will was becoming truly superior to my thinking brain. This resulted in many positive changes to the way I had previously experienced my life, such as: a huge reduction of fear, anger, and worry; a huge increase in making choices that resulted in positive outcomes; being able to see all that I experienced with an educational divine viewpoint; having a devoted love for my spiritual growth that couldn't be compromised; and having an increased sense of confidence that my renewed coexistence with God was going to expand other capabilities of my spirit that were currently unknown to me.

CHAPTER 17

Learning Medical Intuition

The knowledge that is most helpful to our lives is that we have yet to comprehend.

One particular evening, Sarah, Melanie, Ben, and I decided to get together for another insightful conversation at the martial arts studio. For some reason, I felt a guided impulse to arrive a little earlier than scheduled. As a demonstration of my blind faith I did so, which at the very least gave me an opportunity to watch Ben teach his martial arts class. Near the end of the class, Melanie entered the studio and headed toward her office, which was located close to where I was sitting. As I watched her, I unexpectedly began to receive a vision. I saw an image of her veins superimposed upon her body. I could sense that something in regard to her veins or blood was unbalanced or abnormal, but in the moment, I didn't comprehend the meaning behind these images, nor did I understand why I was seeing them.

After the students left the studio, I sat with Melanie and shared my experience with her. I asked if my vision held any significance. She told me that approximately two days ago she'd decided to stop taking her high blood-pressure medication in hopes she no longer needed it. Since then, she could tell that her blood pressure had gotten high again. This was my first experience of being aware of a medical imbalance within another person, an ability that's commonly referred to as medical intuition.

At the time, I had no idea what a medical intuitive was or what one did. I was interested in understanding more about how this ability was connected to my spiritual growth. I had no real knowledge of human anatomy, but after this experience, I had a sincere need to learn more. I purchased a book on the subject and downloaded some related images from the Internet. I wanted to do my part in supporting the path along which I was being guided. My hope was that by being more knowledgeable, it might be easier for me to interpret medically related visions if I ever experienced them again.

At this point, I need to emphasize the importance of exercising free will to do our part in supporting the path along which we are guided. We must take action both to support the path and to appreciate what unfolds as we play an active role in our own lives and spiritual development.

As I compared the process that was allowing me to tap into a constant flow of higher knowledge with the process by which I received medically based knowledge, I was amazed to find that each process was fundamentally the same. In each case, I was using the communication of my spirit to receive knowledge hailing from a source of spiritual energy. In one process, I surrendered myself to the knowledge coming from God's source of spiritual energy; in the other, I surrendered myself to the knowledge coming from Melanie's source of spiritual energy. In each case, the knowledge I received was inspirational, loving, and truthful.

The knowledge I received about Melanie's health helped her become aware that her blood pressure was out of balance; by correcting this, it supported and satisfied her spirit's need to exist in a healthy physical body. In turn, this provided her spirit with a greater opportunity to be more of God, as it lengthened her potential for human existence. The symmetry between these two processes made perfect sense to me. If everyone's spirit comes from God's image, then of course there would be no difference between the communication that occurs between my spirit and God and between my spirit and another spirit created by God. In both instances, by surrendering sole ownership over my spirit, my spirit can unite with another source of spiritual energy and receive knowledge from that source that usually satisfies some spiritual need.

It is the power of spiritual unity that gives my spirit the ability to know what any other source of spiritual energy knows. Through a natural state of spiritual oneness, my spirit can attain unity with any spiritual being. What comes from that spiritual unity is a communication that is always truthful and helpful.

When we place ourselves in a state of spiritual oneness, we access a way of communicating that universally unites all sources of spiritual energy using the same divine visionary language, the power of which is our unconditional love for God and one another. For instance, if I make my spirit aware of medical imbalances within another person, it may communicate words such as blood or heart, which I'd be able to see in my head. From there, I would have to interpret the meaning of such words as they pertained to the medical problem inside that person.

To learn more about medical intuition and to develop this ability, I decided to offer my friends free medical intuition readings. I approached the private readings with the main purpose of nurturing and supporting my own spiritual growth. Remember, it is important to demonstrate a sincere love for our own growth first and foremost. If these opportunities increased the accuracy of my medical awareness, it would benefit any future individuals I provided this service for. *Later on, I would clearly see how valuable this approach would be to my personal happiness.* Living a spiritually centered existence means taking an independent journey toward discovering who I truly am while using the abilities of what I am to create a more enjoyable life. Other people had to be secondary to my own life goals. I had to be steadfast in maintaining support, help, and encouragement toward experiencing my life in the most truthful way I could.

To nurture my own effort to increase the amount of medical information my spirit was capable of receiving, I set an initial goal of being able to receive one single medical validation per reading. From there, with each subsequent reading, I would do my best to increase my accuracy by one. I humbly accepted I was a work-in-progress and maintained a commitment to that approach. I didn't need to relive moments where I fell short in my capabilities. I seemed to be much more compassionate toward myself lately, more willing to learn from the moments when I was successful.

Medical intuition is considered to be a spiritual rarity; having the ability to detect medical imbalances within people is apparently outside the capability of most mediums, psychics, channelers, energy practitioners, and spiritual teachers. Yet I do not feel it should be. The potential of everyone's spirit is equal and without limit; what hinders most of us from self-realizing the extended communication of our spirit is our own mental resistance and undeveloped understanding.

From my experiences with the free medical readings, my medical intuition slowly developed. I progressed from accurately seeing one medical imbalance to more than ten during one sitting. An imbalance could be any change—past or present—in the proper function of one's physical, mental, or spiritual well-being, such as a small skin rash, a mended broken bone, a past surgery, vitamin or mineral deficiencies, a buildup of heavy metals or abnormal cells, abnormal organ function, hormonal imbalances, emotional imbalances, and so on. Over time, I became aware that most of the knowledge I was receiving was already known by whomever I was conducting the reading for. If I sensed someone was experiencing high blood pressure or a heart problem, he or she usually already knew that, privately. Being a student of what I was experiencing, I asked myself: "How can merely extracting information from people that they're already privy to possibly be of help to them?" Many times, I was able to pinpoint medical imbalances that had already been diagnosed by a physician. So, was I really being at all helpful? I asked God: "Why can't I receive new knowledge with the potential to correct or improve someone's current medical problems?"

It wasn't long before I would have a life-changing experience that would validate the potential for my spirit to receive such knowledge. Yet in the meantime, I was learning the importance of not minimizing my spirit's abilities. I didn't feel there were any limitations of my spirit to sense and know helpful information. However, I pinpointed three main sticking points that currently restricted the amount and type of knowledge I could receive. The first was increasing my faith to overcome any resistance of my doubting brain. The second was developing my ability to interpret properly the knowledge received through my spirit. The third was not being personally affected by someone's negative comments or actions.

Doing my part to further the communication of my spirit worked hand in hand with God helping me. I tried to avoid mentally labeling the kind of knowledge my spirit was capable of receiving as either easy or hard, and instead, I viewed all knowledge that my spirit was capable of receiving on the same equal level. One piece of knowledge is not more difficult to receive or more important than any other. All knowledge coming through my spirit has the same intention, which is adding to a person's life by satisfying one's true spiritual needs.

I considered how my effort to satisfy my inner guidance toward understanding more about human anatomy greatly helped improve my medical accuracy. Now, the same guidance was directing me to learn more about natural remedies that improved people's physical, mental, and spiritual imbalances. What I knew about minerals, amino acids, enzymes, and macronutrients was next to nil, but I was determined to do my part to find out how they contributed to our health.

Cancer, in particular, interested me, and I wondered if there was something I might be able to do to prevent it. I had a sense there was a limited "window of opportunity" for me with regard to this interest. Even though I wasn't completely sure what this meant, I was aware that if something was heading my way, I was going to be ready for it.

CHAPTER 18

My First Conversation with a Spirit

While there will always be moments when we will be able to act with courage, not all of us will choose to live our lives courageously.

As time went on, I encountered a progressive series of experiences that not only concretely validated the guidance received by my spirit but resulted in outcomes I believed represented small personal miracles. Personal miracles are divinely responsible enlightening occurrences that everyone has the potential to experience. Each of us has multiple opportunities during our lifetime to experience personal miracles; they are not as rare as most people believe. What is rare is our faith in our inner guidance that causes these personal miracles to happen for us.

My first experience communicating with the spirit of a once-living human being happened very unexpectedly. I was in my living room one evening when I became aware of what felt like a spiritual presence. Up until this point, the knowledge that came through my spirit either originated from a loving source of higher wisdom or medical knowledge that originated from a living, breathing human being. Along with my Catholic upbringing came an investment in the existence of evil beings such as Satan and demons, so when the spiritual presence first encountered me, I was concerned it might not possess loving intentions. But of all the knowledge that had been shared with me so far, none hinted at the existence of pure evil, and I had never personally sensed a spiritual presence of pure evil, either.

Determined to be a good student of God, I slipped into a state of spiritual oneness and surrendered myself to any knowledge I hoped this spirit wanted to communicate. The spirit told me that he was once a human male and had a message for someone I knew personally. He said he had been like a brother to this person, and at times, he'd taken on a paternal role toward her. He had suffered a disease that had caused him and his family much pain. He regretted the disease had taken his life, and was sorry he hadn't lived up to his responsibility of taking better care of himself. He wanted me to know that he had "heard what she said," and it was because of what "she" said that he was here in spirit, communicating with me. The last bit of knowledge I received was that he was connected to a friend of Michelle's named Tara. I only vaguely knew Tara; she was someone I hadn't seen or spoken to in a few years. I wasn't quite sure what my next move would be with the information I'd been given, but I was afraid it could result in a painful experience.

While I sensed what the spirit had told me was the truth, I still wasn't absolutely sure. Tara and her family had been my parents' neighbors for several years, and Michelle had experienced a much closer relationship with Tara than I ever had. A plethora of mental fears crept into my thoughts as I wondered whether to get in touch with Tara. Could I have a conversation with a woman I barely knew about subject matter she might likely resist and still have it turn out in a positive way? Other fears included wondering whether the knowledge would make any sense to her, and if what the spirit was communicating was not true, how might Tara and others view me after I conveyed it? If I did decide to contact Tara, I would have to call Michelle for her phone number, and thus, explain my reasons for calling Tara in the first place. Michelle herself probably had all the reason in the world to consider me a nutcase and my concerns ludicrous. Only a few people knew about the new way of life I was pursuing. Even though I was making a strong effort to fully understand what I was experiencing, I knew I lacked the proper words to explain it well to others who were outside of my small circle of friends. This included many members of my immediate and extended family.

Despite my mental torment, I knew how very necessary it was for me to demonstrate a strong faith in the communication I'd experienced. I viewed it as a great opportunity to validate a life lesson that had been previously shared with me. This life lesson involved surrendering control over my life to any knowledge or guidance that came from a loving spiritual source. While this male spirit was not part of the higher wisdom I was used to placing my trust in, I did sense that the spirit's knowledge and what the spirit wished me to do were loving and sincere. What I understood, so far, was that I was having experiences to learn more about a universal way of life based on unconditional love. It was crucial that I did not waver from my co-partnership with God. My role in this co-partnership was to demonstrate blind faith in God and pursue the various forms of guidance that were being communicated to my spirit. After following whatever my inner guidance directed me to do, I was simply meant to sit back and watch it all naturally unfold into a loving experience. If this experience had been divinely shifted into my life, then it was up to me to do my part to help fulfill its purpose.

So, I went ahead and called Michelle, who was one of the few people aware of the positive developments occurring in my life. Yet as spirit communication was only happening to me for the first time, I wasn't sure what Michelle's reaction would be. I could begin my story with something such as "to my surprise," but it wouldn't be true. I cannot recall a single family member who didn't react to my experiences with doubt, disbelief, or cynicism. (My brother went so far as to suggest I had experienced a severe nervous breakdown.) While Michelle might not have understood everything I was experiencing or accepted it as fact, she was likely the most open-minded of everyone around me.

So, Michelle supported my decision to call Tara, but she reminded me that Tara's husband was a devout atheist and that Tara herself shared a similar viewpoint. I literally became nauseous at the idea of following through with the call. After providing me with Tara's phone number, Michelle once again supported me in my decision and wished me luck.

I truly wished I had some spiritual sense of how this was all about to unfold, but I didn't. I was just hoping that my new perspective about love and God was accurate, and that this particular situation would result in an experience that I would one day reflect upon with pride.

The phone rang several times before Tara answered. In a way, I saw this as a good starting point, because there were three other people in her household who could have picked up the phone. I began the conversation by identifying who I was. I addressed the fact that it had been years since she and I had last talked, and I explained I was nervous about the information I was about to share with her, and if she felt uncomfortable at any time to please tell me, and I would immediately stop speaking.

I began with a brief explanation of the way of life I was currently experiencing, which I'd recently realized allowed me to receive messages from spirits on the "other side." I told Tara that the information I was about to convey to her came from a family member of hers who had passed away. Her immediate response was one of mixed emotion; even though there was an obvious reluctance in her voice, I sensed she was still willing to listen to what I had to share. I began by laying the ground-work of how I saw myself as a work in progress; that the information I was about to share with her—if it were true—would require her help to make sense of it all. She agreed.

I began by sharing with her that if I had accurately interpreted what the spirit was saying, the spirit was a male family member of hers with whom she had been very close. The male spirit had shared some knowledge about how he had been like both a brother and a father to Tara. Even though the information didn't make much sense to me personally, I took Tara's silence as a sign of support and continued on with my account. I said how the spirit told me he'd been sick with the same illness suffered by another person in his family; that this disease had taken his life; and that he regretted it. He had also spoken about not living up to some responsibility he felt he'd had regarding her. I briefly paused to give Tara some space, but all I heard was silence. I finished by sharing with Tara that the spirit ended the communication by saying something about how he had "heard her" and that was why he had approached me.

Contrary to my numerous mental fears and doubts, Tara provided me with the following "decoding" of the information I'd shared with her: The disease of alcoholism was prevalent in her family, and her brother Scott, an alcoholic, had ultimately lost his battle to it at an early age. He had indeed taken on a paternal role with her and would often promise her he would do his best to prevent his addiction from taking over his life. The day before my conversation with Scott's spirit and with Tara herself, Tara had actually been thinking about Scott and silently asked him for some sign that he was all right.

I thanked Tara for being so helpful and supportive. In response, she thanked me for having the courage to share my experience with her. She said it gave her hope that Scott was still in her life and at peace.

I was overjoyed. The spirit I had communicated with wasn't just any spirit who happened to "stop by" but one with a meaningful message for a specific person. This spirit was aware of and responded to his sister's private and sincere request. It made sense that because the essence of love had connected these two people in life, it continued to connect them in the afterlife. But what was confusing and perplexing to me at the time was how it was possible for Scott's spirit to be aware of my capacity to receive and convey his messages to his sister.

Then I thought about the state of spiritual oneness. In such a state, a sincere, loving need fuses a connection between spirits. The divine strength of a sincere, loving need has the power to make a spirit in a physical body (mine) and a spirit without a physical body (Scott) aware of each other in order to be helpful to each other. In this particular case, it was the divine communication of love that not only allowed Scott to discern his sister's sincere need but to connect his spirit with mine. Interestingly, the divine communication responsible for this experience was extremely similar to my recent experience of having my spirit suddenly and loving guided to a specific location at the Hamilton Police Department, where I had seen the emotionally upset woman, Cindy, in sincere need of a loving gesture on my part.

Above anything else, it was my faith and courage that allowed me to open the door to these two amazing and beautiful experiences. How many times in the past had my lack of faith and mental fears talked me out of listening to the ability of my spirit to sense, know, and understand the truthful path my life needed to take? As a result, how many amazing and beautiful experiences had I inadvertently barred from my life? I discovered that fear is a response my brain expresses whenever it thinks it cannot control the outcome of a situation in the positive way it wants for itself. My new philosophy was proving that following the communication of my spirit resulted in amazing, loving experiences while disproving my mental fears. I knew that during my lifetime, there would always be moments when I would need to act with courage, but for the time being, I was beginning to understand what it meant to live my life *courageously*.

CHAPTER 19

My Spiritual Connection to God

Our spiritual progression and success
are dependent on truthful change.

As a child, I was taught to believe in heaven, God, Jesus, and the Holy Spirit as well as demons, hell, and Satan. Due to this past belief, in the early stages of my spiritual development, I was unsure whether using the communication of my spirit could result in connecting with a demon or pure evil in spirit form. But my endeavor toward universal truth was all about challenging my previously accepted core beliefs to attain a more divine perspective. This transformation of perspective mainly allowed me to view myself as a spirit who was created from a universal, loving God.

If my spirit and everyone else's spirit was truly created from the spiritual image of God, then the soul of God is eternally part of everyone's spirit. If the spirit of all things is created from the spiritual image of God; possesses the soul of God; and is always influenced by the power of God's love; then pure evil cannot exist. In my eyes, pure evil meant any spirit not created from the spiritual image of God and immune to the power of God's love. Even though there was already an unbreakable bond between everyone's spirit and the loving soul of God, during our human existence God purposely gave everyone's spirit the freedom to choose how loving it wishes to be. Every spirit will always be influenced and affected by the power of love; no spirit can prevent that from happening. (Yet if I were mistaken, then I was sure opening myself up to unchangeable negative energies, something I could greatly regret!)

To validate this, I allowed myself to be influenced by information from any and all spirits that I sensed had a sincere, loving message. At the same time, I would be enthusiastic to learn more about unloving spirits, should I come into contact with any. I believed most unloving spirits were nothing more than those of ordinary people who had chosen to lead an unloving existence during their time on Earth; hence the unloving ways they'd lived had followed them into the afterlife. That did not mean, however, that unloving spirits represented pure evil. As with everything related to my new endeavor, I sought to validate my beliefs by demonstrating faith in them to prove their legitimacy.

If my understanding was truly accurate, it would be enlightening to continuously encounter spirits that always possess at least some essence of love within them, no matter how minimally. I was eager for more opportunities to speak with spirits and to learn more about their life on the other side. I again sought help from Sarah, Melanie, and Ben, requesting that they connect me with any friends who might possibly be interested in a free spiritual session. They were very accommodating and helpful in scheduling opportunities for medical readings and\or the delivery of messages from spirits of passed loved ones. I arranged to provide these sessions at the martial arts studio, the public library, the local Starbucks, my apartment, or people's homes. At the time, it didn't matter where meetings with other people took place; I was simply grateful and thankful for any opportunity to further my education. When I wasn't working or spending time with my daughter, I enjoyed every chance to better understand and expand the language of my spirit.

At the same time, I remained focused on improving my medical knowledge and began to use holistic solutions for certain medical problems I spiritually sensed in others as well as myself. For about four months, I noticed a lump had been developing on the inside of my mouth. At first it didn't alarm me, but then it increased in size from week to week. If anything, it started as a persistent nuisance that was most noticeable whenever I chewed. It developed into a sizeable-enough lump that I considered contacting a doctor. Yet while researching different kinds of herbs, I decided to make a few tinctures and extracts and turn to those holistic options for help first. For a reason I was not aware of at the time, I was quite preoccupied with one herb in particular: bloodroot. It was often used to rid the body of certain types of cancerous cells. I purchased a small quantity of this herb from a reputable source, sensing a strong need that I should begin taking it.

Approximately a week after I ingested the bloodroot, something very unusual occurred. One morning as I headed into my kitchen to check the weather out the window, I realized the lump had gotten much larger. I rushed to the bathroom mirror and gently maneuvered the left side of my mouth into a position where I could more easily see inside it. That's when I heard a noticeable pop and felt a small mass resting inside the walls of my mouth that I spit out into the sink. A small yet visible hole now existed at the exact place the lump of tissue had been. I had never seen anything like it before and haven't since, nor have I ever experienced my body undergoing such a "removal process." While I would not be able to prove it, I couldn't help but wonder if I might have eliminated a cancerous growth from my body and prevented my body from further harm.

Soon after, I recalled the previous inner knowing or sense of having a "window of opportunity" to learn about the health of the human body, a process that led me to this specific herb. I then accepted the validation that this inner knowing or sense proved itself by leading me to a remedy to rid my body of a potentially harmful mass before it became a health risk. If I had any doubts about the validation of what I just experienced, they would be wholly erased by what followed next. Within a short time, I would become involved in yet another health-related situation—an even more serious one where the remedy and knowledge I had been inspired with would assist two people with a desperate need for physical and spiritual healing.

CHAPTER 20

A Son's Faith Overcomes His Father's Cancer

Viewing others not as our possessions but more as guests in our lives encourages us to act in a much more grateful and thankful way toward one another.

Approximately three weeks after the mass was organically forced from my body, I was making tea in my kitchen when I sensed the presence of a spirit in the room. I immediately ceased my activities and focused my awareness on the spirit and any information it wished to share. Several minutes passed before I could sense that this was a female spirit who had been a blood relation of my friend, Ben. The first image that the female spirit influenced me with was of her weeping. The interpretation I received of this image was that the female spirit was saddened by a situation that was currently occurring within her living family. (I don't feel that spirits actually shed tears and cry; I believe they create images to help me understand the real meaning they wish to convey.) Then the female spirit shared additional images with me. One was of a train that operated close to her home. Another image involved the name Ann, which could indeed be her first name, but it could just as easily be the first name of someone meaningful to her about whom she wished to speak. I also felt a very strong sense of the female spirit wanting me to contact Ben immediately. Even though Ben was my friend, Ben came from an unloving upbringing through which he learned to be self-reliant, not to accept help from others, and the importance of keeping others from knowing personal information about him and his family. Even though I knew Ben kept his family situations closely guarded, I still followed the spirit's guidance by picking up my cell phone and calling him. After several rings, Ben answered his phone. I first asked if he was available to speak and, said that if so, I had some messages for him to validate that I believed were coming from a female spirit associated with his family. In an uncharacteristically hushed voice, Ben said he could spare a moment for me. I responded by slowly repeating the information and understanding conveyed to me by the female spirit. When I finished, Ben said he understood everything I had shared with him. He continued by saying that his father had a sister named Ann who had passed away several years ago. Ben's aunt Ann had lived in a community with a large train station, and he remembered taking the train as a child to visit her, as her home was only a brief walk from the station. Ben said he knew why Aunt Ann was upset. He was presently in the waiting room of a hospital in Philadelphia with his entire family, as his father, John, was gravely ill. Right before my phone call, he and his family had met with the doctor who had just completed a procedure to remove a cancerous tumor. The doctor had informed the family that during the procedure, it was apparent the cancer had spread to other organs; as a result, he and his team decided not to continue the surgery. The doctor then informed the family that John, who was in his late seventies, had stage IV pancreatic cancer with a life expectancy of four to eight weeks. Ben was distraught, despite his attempt to maintain a tough persona about it all; the sadness inevitably crept into his voice. I apologized to him for the timing of my phone call, but he responded with words of compassion and understanding, assuring me that it had been the right decision to call him.

I didn't know this at the time, but my strong sense to take a "health day" from work the next morning was actually a guiding hand, creating an opportunity to be helpful to Ben. In the past, I would have suppressed this sense by allowing my reasoning to dissuade me. If I had acted similarly in this case, it would have prevented me from experiencing the personal miracle this act of faith ended up initiating.

I was sincerely grateful for my job at the police department and very proud of my career. While working in an undercover capacity, my hours always varied to correspond with the irregular hours of drug dealers. Often, I would be given "personal hours" instead of overtime monies to compensate for working extended hours. My accrued personal time allowed me to take days off without much prior notice.

Not fully knowing how my day would unfold, I simply entrusted my life to the more spontaneous direction that living in the moment requires. My new way of experiencing life often guided me to alter or change my normal routines to fulfill a future purpose not yet known to me. Blind faith is all about surrendering control over our lives to fulfill a higher purpose not yet known.

I spent a good portion of my day off performing the usual duties around my home, such as cooking and cleaning. I also took a walk in a nearby park to enjoy the open air and natural surroundings. When I returned, I comfortably positioned myself on my couch in preparation to receive any wisdom that might make itself available to me. I made myself quiet; put myself in a state of deep peace; and enjoyed the experience of spiritual stillness and oneness. I surrendered my awareness to any messages, knowledge, or insights that wished to make themselves known to me.

Almost immediately, I became spiritually aware of John, Ben's father. While deepening my awareness of him, I was inspired with images of the herb I had taken that may have caused the unknown mass to dislodge from my mouth. Then I began to see visions of oxygen being delivered into my lungs while also being inspired with the understanding that God created the physical body to have a healthy oxygen level. I could see images of how oxygen runs through our veins, arteries, and capillaries so it can be delivered to the brain, organs, and tissue; I saw images of the heart and how it pumps oxygenated blood for the rest of the body to use.

From these images, I became aware of other organs, specifically the stomach. While viewing images of the stomach and the digestion process, I considered the importance of our bodies' enzymes and how crucial they are to the function of our bodies. For nearly an hour, I received images I didn't fully understand the meaning of, but they all involved the importance of oxygen within the body; the need for additional oxygen in certain situations; the fact that enzymes improve how the body functions; and the natural herb that I felt was responsible for dislodging the unknown mass from my mouth.

When I felt I'd learned everything I was capable of in that particular moment, I again turned to certain credible resources over the Internet to help me understand more about the knowledge I had just received. I found that the pancreas creates enzymes that the body uses to combat diseased cells and digest food, which made sense of the images regarding the digestive system that I'd seen. It stood to reason that John's pancreas was being prevented from generating the enzymes his body needed to function properly. I meticulously wrote all these details down in a simple and straightforward way with the intention of presenting them to Ben.

About a day later, our group arranged to meet at the martial arts club for one of our bimonthly meetings. I was the first to arrive, and soon afterward I saw Ben. Ben had taken on a leadership role in his family's life. I had no doubt that if he thought that this was the right course of action for his father, he was going to make a sincere effort to make it happen on his own.

I had established credibility with Ben that the knowledge I was spiritually receiving was truthful. I presented him with the health-related information I'd written down for him, which included the name of the herb I'd taken; the type of enzymes I thought might be relevant to his father's predicament; what food grade liquid oxygen was; and where and how to purchase those items. After listening intently, Ben thanked me, and we went on with an enjoyable evening discussion.

The next day, Ben placed an order for all the items I had suggested. Later in the week, Ben met with John's doctors, who had John on heavy doses of pain medication to make the remaining days of his life as pleasant as possible. Ben confided with the doctors about his interest in administering alternative and holistic medicine to his dad in hopes it could be helpful. The doctors assured Ben there was no chance John's condition could be reversed, but if he chose to use alternative treatments, that was fine with them.

Ben's next step was convincing John to accept the treatment. The lengthy conversation he had with his father on this matter resulted in a much better outcome than he'd ever expected. Ben and John had not been close while Ben was growing up. The family was large and had very little money, and many unresolved personal issues between family members remained unsettled. It had always been difficult for John to accept help from people, even from his own family. But with nothing to lose, John agreed to accept Ben's help.

Over the next four weeks, Ben made a sincere effort to reorganize his life so he could help administer John's alternative treatment. Things Ben had previously filled his life with were now being replaced with something of considerable, loving importance. Ben's goal was to make the most heartfelt attempt to do all that he was capable of to help his father.

Our personal faith in a higher wisdom needs to be demonstrated to be proven. By overcoming our mental resistance to demonstrate faith in our inner guidance, we create opportunities for God to reveal how miraculous life can be when we do it together. By maintaining a spiritually centered existence, we give God an opportunity to demonstrate and prove just how much we don't know.

After the first week John diligently took the alternative health treatments, he began to regain strength. Color was slowly returning to his face; his appetite was increasing; and he was able to sit up in bed. By the end of the second week, John's strength and energy continued to improve, and with Ben's agreement, he returned home. A few days later, he showed enough strength to stand and maintain a conversation for much longer spans of time. By the end of the third week, John was walking around and returning to the routines of his house that he loved, particularly attending to his garden, where Ben would now find him most of the time. John's energy continued to improve and was eventually restored.

After about six weeks, John was scheduled for another test to determine how much the cancer had grown or not. After the tests were concluded and then rechecked, the physician met with Ben. During their conversation, the physician stated that the tests revealed a quantity of cancer cells that were below the level of any health concern. The physician explained to Ben that, miraculously, it wasn't that the cancer was in remission—it was simply no longer there.

John was now physically capable of returning to the quality of life he'd originally enjoyed. For the next four years, Ben visited his father regularly throughout the week, keeping an eye on his dad's health while enjoying his company. After one of his visits, Ben promised his father he would return the next day to help him with a home-improvement project. When Ben arrived at his father's house, he found his father lying dead on the living room floor. John was fully clothed as if he was ready for a day's work in his garden. John's sudden passing affected Ben deeply, yet he was very grateful for the time they had spent together. During John and Ben's renewed relationship, Ben had often told me how his father frequently gave him credit for saving his life, and this belief had enabled father and son to have a better relationship than ever before.

Before John's passing, John and Ben spoke much more openly and truthfully with each other about past family issues and experiences that they had previously found too difficult to discuss. From these conversations, Ben received the opportunity to have more of an open, loving relationship with his father, just as John had more of an opportunity to be a father to Ben in the way that Ben had always deserved.

I did not believe the alternative remedy I was inspired with had the potential to cure all advanced cases of pancreatic cancer, but it miraculously cured this one. Not only had that knowledge helped cure Ben's father of cancer—it gave father and son another opportunity to create a bond of love that will keep them eternally united with each other.

The way I understood God explaining this miraculous experience to me was: Never minimize the capability of your spirit, and never minimize what we are capable of doing together. We are just beginning.

CHAPTER 21

The Love Triangle

We must learn how to voice ourselves in a truthful and loving way, especially during moments of personal adversity.

There were now many noticeable changes in the way I was living. Living more in the moment slowed down my pace considerably. I continued to experience a much stronger spiritual will that gave me the needed strength and confidence to accomplish any goals I was being divinely guided to pursue. At the same time, my efforts to remain spiritually centered and regain the natural alignment of "Spirit, Mind, Body" drained my energy, as my body was not yet accustomed to it. This period of energetic adjustment lasted for many months, if not a few years. Often this energy drain increased my need for sleep; I slept more frequently and for longer periods. Eventually, the energy drain did lift, but it took time, and I was able to be patient with it. In the past, if I had made efforts to change myself and change hadn't occurred in the short time frame that I mentally wanted, I would come up with reasons to stop. Now, a stronger spirit helped me stay committed not only to truthful change but to the truth, especially during moments of personal adversity. This was exactly what I needed to have in place in order to satisfy the next challenge that confronted me.

Melanie asked me to provide a private reading for her longtime friend, Donna, as there was a specific individual who had passed away with whom Donna wished to communicate. Once again, by providing free personal readings for people, I felt I was doing my part to create opportunities for myself to grow spiritually. As helpful as my readings were to others, they also allowed me to improve the accuracy of the knowledge I received, communicate that knowledge in a loving way, and expand my understanding of the language of my spirit.

Whenever I was asked to communicate with someone's loved one in spirit, I would insist on having very little knowledge about the spirit or about the living person requesting the reading. Prior to her friend's reading, the only two pieces of information I permitted Melanie to share with me were her friend Donna's first name and the fact that Donna wished to communicate with the spirit of her deceased husband.

Upon my arrival at Melanie's home, I was led into her dining room. Donna was sitting in a chair at the dining room table, and it was apparent she was eagerly hoping and waiting to receive messages from the spirit of her husband.

All my readings began with a twofold approach: First, I considered myself grateful to connect with any spirit that wished to communicate with me. Second, I hoped to receive insight from that spirit to satisfy a spiritual need for his or her living loved one. I was firm with whomever I read for that my primary role was to be more of an educator of the spiritual side of life than anything else. In other words, my role was to honor and to, as accurately as I could, convey the messages communicated to my spirit. My concern was less about getting the approval or acknowledgement of the person(s) in front of me. In this way, my not being preoccupied or tied to an outcome of approval freed me to allow my spirit priority over my thinking brain. In my pursuit to prove the existence of the higher wisdom of God, I always believed that the spirits of our loved ones were capable of providing us with a great deal of insightful knowledge. The content of such insightful knowledge may not have been what we were looking for or expecting, but that was just the point in that we should not have an expectation and not allow our thinking brain to distort, color, or influence the messages of spirit.

I sat at a dining room table across from Donna. Nervous, Donna requested that Melanie sit at the same table with us. I began the session by asking Donna to allow me initially to share information I received from any spirit without interruptions, and that, at some point, I would pause to ask her what information I was receiving made sense to her and what didn't. I also told Donna that my job was to communicate only the truth; I would never attempt to make any information "fit" or attempt to convince her I was right.

To begin with, I explained to Donna that on Earth, our spirit is placed in a physical body to have human experiences. One day, our physical bodies and physical brains are no longer able to sustain life. When this happens, our spirit ascends from its human existence and is no longer affected by physical limitations—it can no longer use its thinking brain as its source of knowledge and guidance. Spirits do not think. On earth, our own spirit always senses and knows the loving and truthful thing to say or do, but often, our thinking brain convinces us not to follow that spiritual choice. After our spirit ascends from its physical existence, it becomes connected to a strong source of unconditional love, which greatly influences our spirit always to speak the truth and communicate itself in a loving way. It will bear witness to every moment of its existence on Earth in a truthful way. For the very first time, our spirit will observe the life it created for itself on Earth, all the loving moments and all the unloving moments. It will witness the loving choices it made for itself and toward others as well as all the unloving choices that hindered its life and the lives of others. This experience to see itself in a truthful way greatly humbles all spirits. Lastly, spirits will usually speak about themselves, their lives, and their new truthful perspectives, and not from the perspectives they had during their human existence.

After I shared my guidelines with Donna, she nodded in agreement. Several moments later, I began to sense the presence of a male spirit. I told Donna that this male spirit felt more like a friend to Donna than a family member. For the next fifteen minutes, I relayed the following knowledge to Donna that the male spirit communicated to me: The male spirit said he had known Donna in high school, and they had briefly dated, despite a three- to four-year age difference between them. The male spirit acknowledged that he had truly loved Donna, but it had been difficult for her to accept his love. In addition, Donna's parents had not openly accepted their relationship because of their difference in age. He communicated that he had loved Donna for many years and still loved her to this day, even admitting that he was a die-hard romantic. He related a story about his once having arranged a surprise picnic for himself and Donna. Finally, the male spirit communicated that the first name Tom was significant.

I paused my conversation with the male spirit to ask Donna if any of the information I'd relayed made sense. Without hesitation, the woman quickly stated that no, none of the knowledge I shared with her made one iota of sense.

These are the moments that create great opportunities for us to see for ourselves the level of real faith and trust that we have in the knowledge our spirit receives.

With growing confusion, I asked Donna if she was sure. Donna nodded and said, "Yes, I'm sure."

I turned to Melanie and somehow found the faith and self-courage to inform her calmly, "Donna is lying." Donna argued that she wasn't. To verify what I spiritually sensed was the truth, I asked Donna individual questions about the conversation I'd just had with the male spirit. To begin with, I asked Donna if she'd had a boyfriend during high school who had been three or four years older.

"Yes," she responded, hesitantly. I then asked whether her parents had a difficult time accepting the age difference between her and the boyfriend. Donna slowly responded that yes, her parents had a very difficult time and even encouraged her not to date him. I asked Donna about the picnic, and she admitted that her boyfriend had once met her outside after school, guided her to a secluded location on school grounds, and laid out a blanket with food he'd prepared for them to share. I asked Donna if she believed this man had loved her and if he'd ever expressed that love. Donna confirmed yes to both inquiries and went on to state that, because of her parents' resistance, she had ended the relationship. For years afterward, this man sent her letters, sometimes poems, even after she met her eventual husband and married. In his letters, her old boyfriend would write about his life and even his own marriage to another woman, but he would always refer to Donna as his one true love. Donna continued to receive his letters up until a few years ago, having secretly kept and hidden them from her husband, who had recently passed away. I asked Donna the name of her high school boyfriend, and, not surprisingly, she responded: "It was Tom."

Melanie asked Donna why she hadn't initially told the truth about Tom. Donna said she'd requested this reading with me in order to communicate with her deceased husband, Sam, whom she had loved dearly. Donna had covered up the story about Tom for fear that Sam would find out she had been secretly keeping Tom's love letters all these years and hadn't told him.

A few minutes later, I was able to communicate with Sam's spirit, and his response about Tom was just the opposite of what Donna had feared it would be. Sam's spirit made Donna aware that in his new existence, he was now capable of seeing the truth about anything Donna had previously hidden from him. Sam's spirit explained that the love he now experiences has changed his earthly perspective for the better. Sam's spirit shared that he now sees how other people are not our possessions, and no one is born into this life with a permanent obligation to share his or her life with someone else. Sam spoke about seeing everyone as a spiritual guest in another's life. Seeing his relationship with Donna from this new perspective, Sam did not find fault with Donna's actions to keep and hide the letters; instead, he used his time to communicate all the ways over the many years that Donna had added to his life, expressing how grateful he was that she had chosen to do so.

After the reading, I returned home and reflected upon the experience I'd just had. My transformation toward a more spiritually centered existence had decreased the influence my fears and doubts once had on me. In the past, I never would have had the faith to tell someone I'd just met for the first time that she was lying, especially after she told me she wasn't, and expect it to produce a loving outcome. In my education to be more of God, I understood that the sudden sense of pride I received from this experience was actually a universal response God purposely created to emerge whenever people demonstrate the self-courage to overcome a moment of personal adversity by making wise choices that produce loving outcomes.

CHAPTER 22

Love Found in a
Silver Pocket Watch

*Love is the proof that we are all
spiritually equal.*

One afternoon in December 2006, Michelle and I were discussing our Christmas plans in the kitchen of her townhouse in Hamilton, New Jersey. During our conversation, I became aware of the presence of her father, Charlie, who'd passed after a heart attack several years earlier in the kitchen of his home in Florida. Michelle immediately noticed what had become more familiar to her as of late—namely, a change in my attention and that telltale blank stare on my face that meant I was in communication with a spirit. Prior to this occasion, I'd had several conversations with Charlie's spirit, which enjoyed sharing insight from the perspective of his "new existence." Charlie's spirit had shared insightful information with Michelle as well as with other members of his living family, including a more enlightened understanding of what had caused certain family relationships to deteriorate. Charlie had been a huge Elvis Presley fan; he once owned many of Elvis's albums and could be caught singing the King's songs out loud when he didn't think anyone was listening.

While Charlie's spirit was communicating with me, my twelve-year-old daughter, Courtney, walked into the kitchen. Understanding that I was communicating with a spirit, Courtney asked her mom whom I was speaking with. During these early stages of my endeavor, it had been amazing to witness how supportive and accepting Courtney had been about the changes taking place in my life. Michelle explained to Courtney that I was communicating with the spirit of her grandfather. Without hesitation, Courtney greeted Charlie with an enthusiastic "Hi, Grandpop!" I could sense how elated Charlie was by the presence of his granddaughter, especially when he shared the image of his face smiling with me.

Charlie's spirit requested that I ask Courtney what she would love for Christmas. After I relayed the question to her, Courtney immediately acknowledged that ever since she was little, she'd had a hidden desire to own an old, silver pocket watch. Admittedly, such a unique request took Michelle and me completely by surprise. Not once had Courtney ever before mentioned a loving desire to own such an item. The sudden response I then received from Charlie caused me absolute disbelief and awe. Through a combination of imagery, words, and feelings, Charlie proceeded to share with me precise details about a specific old, silver pocket watch and where it was located. The knowledge Charlie inspired me with took all of several seconds, but I knew it would take me a while to explain everything to Michelle and Courtney.

Charlie's spirit showed me an overhead view of a roadway leading into the town of New Hope, Pennsylvania. I was familiar with the town from visiting it in the past; it was a well-known tourist town where a wide variety of independently owned clothing shops, restaurants, entertainment, retail goods, and personal services were located. He then led me down the roadway to a bridge that crossed the Delaware River, directing me to the right side of the road where an abandoned store sat on the corner. Charlie then directed me toward a row of stores that were ultimately connected to the abandoned one. He made me aware of the third store from the abandoned one and told me it was a jewelry store, one that sold watches. I saw an older man inside the store; he looked approximately sixty years old, very thin, and he had a full head of grey hair. I felt certain he was the store owner. I also saw a cane hanging in the corner of the store, but it seemed to belong to someone other than the old man. Finally, I saw a silver pocket watch in a display case. Charlie stated that it would cost around $210 and had been made in the early 1890s, being previously owned by a man who had lovingly passed it down to his son before he died. Charlie smiled once more before his presence slowly faded from my awareness. In his departing moments, he let me know it was now up to Michelle and me to do our part together, not separately, in obtaining the watch for Courtney.

To be completely honest, I was quite skeptical that my interpretation of the information I had received was completely accurate. I was still very new to communicating with spirits, and because of that, my ability to interpret properly every detail that Charlie's spirit was communicating to me was questionable. Being a constant student of what I had been experiencing, I knew my role was to fully understand the divine language that makes this all possible. Yet, I also knew I was years away from fulfilling that role. As I've discussed, our ability to communicate with other sources of spiritual energy is not as out of reach as most people think it is. One of my constant challenges was having unconditional faith in the unusual or out-of-norm knowledge that I spiritually received. Because my connection with Charlie's spirit was strong, the next step was making a sincere effort to validate the information I'd received.

A few days later, unbeknownst to our daughter, Michelle and I took a car trip to New Hope. Once we arrived, we reduced our driving speed, as neither of us was too familiar with the layout of the town. We both kept an eye out for any abandoned corner store situated on the right side of the road. We soon approached an intersection on the main town road, and what we saw pleasantly surprised us. There on the most right-hand corner of the road, just as Charlie had promised, was an abandoned store. After parking in a lot, we headed to the store, stopped when we reached it, and counted three shops down to find a very small jewelry store.

In the spirit of the season, the store was decked out with holiday décor, and Christmas music was playing. The shop itself was tiny, but there were plenty of glass cabinets and display cases to explore. A man then emerged from a back room and approached one of his customers with a necklace of some sort. His appearance was exactly as Charlie had described—he had a full head of grey hair, he seemed about sixty years old, and he was very slender. Soon he approached and greeted Michelle and me, inquiring as to whether we were looking for anything specific. With a nervous smile, I asked him if there was any chance he sold pocket watches. He said he did, and not only that, but he was one of the very rare store owners in New Hope who sold them. He headed over to a glass display case and let us know he only had about five left. I asked if any were silver. He pointed to the top of the display case and announced that just one was silver; the rest were gold and copper.

As he removed the silver pocket watch from the case, I asked if he knew the watch's origin. He said it had been made around the early 1900s, that he had obtained it from an estate sale, and, if he remembered correctly, the gentleman who previously owned it had passed away and his family had sold it to the store when they were parting with some of his other belongings they didn't wish to keep. The salesman wasn't entirely positive how that gentleman came to receive the watch, but he said that quite often watches of this type were passed down from father to son. This was simply amazing to Michelle and me! Eagerly, I asked the salesman what price he had placed on the silver pocket watch. He checked its tag and told me $210, the exact amount Charlie had said it would be. While Michelle and I beamed at each other, we happily told the salesman we would take it.

As the salesman lightly polished the watch for us, Michelle and I looked around for any type of walking cane but saw none. I began a conversation with the salesman, hoping to learn a little bit more about him and his business. He explained that the store wasn't just his, but his wife's, too, and they had owned and operated the business for many years. Due to an unforeseen illness, his wife was unable to walk or work, and he said he missed having her around the store. This explained why I saw the cane. I was learning that some visions, such as the one I had of the cane, are not to be taken literally but are created to shed more meaning to the overall story. My interpretation of what the visions are trying to communicate to me is key. I now saw what the vision was attempting to communicate to me from the start. I was meant to put together a story as to why there was a cane inside the store that was not the male store owner's, why it was hanging in the interior of the store and not somewhere else, and why I sensed the true owner of the cane was not able to be there to use it. The simple vision of this lonely cane was attempting to tell me how much a man missed the many years of loving experiences he had with his wife while sharing the responsibilities of the store together.

At that very moment, "I'll Be Home for Christmas" began playing—and not just any rendition, but Elvis Presley's. Michelle and I grinned at one another. Of course, we both knew what the other was thinking: this incredible, magical story that Michelle and I were guided to experience together was Charlie's Christmas gift to us, and he got to witness it all.

On Christmas Day, Courtney received the watch—the gift the spirit of her grandfather had given to her. Her eyes brimmed with tears as she held the silver pocket watch in her hands, constantly turning it to examine it from different angles. For the next hour, Michelle and I shared every detail of the heartfelt experience her grandfather's spirit guided us on, a guidance that led us not only to the gift that Courtney specifically stated she had a secret love for but to a loving experience that deeply affected Michelle and me. Recounting this inspiring story that Charlie's spirit blessed our lives with has become a Christmas tradition for our family.

Our spirit's abilities will help us discover a whole new way to experience our lives. This experience was a great education for me. The afterlife that everyone's spirit will one day ascend to is governed by and influenced by the same power of unconditional love that influences and governs all people's lives during their human existence. The difference is that Charlie's spirit no longer has a thinking brain offering its resistance toward communicating the truth or acting in an unconditionally loving way. During our human existence, our mental wants will strongly resists our spirit's desire to naturally speak the truth and act in unconditionally loving ways. The power of wanting money is a strong influence in our human society. This power encourages and influences daily competition among people rather than a harmony of existence. Our ascended society is based on the divine power of love and a truthful view of ourselves. Being a student of this experience, I became aware of the vast amounts of knowledge Charlie's spirit could have shared with his granddaughter but didn't. Charlie's spirit specifically asked his granddaughter the question, "What would you love for Christmas?" In response, Courtney shared a hidden natural love for an old silver pocket watch without knowing why she had that love for it. In turn, Charlie encouraged Michelle and me to follow his instructions together and not separately. This amazing series of events strongly validated for me that the universal communication of love is really divine guidance that directs everyone toward loving experiences with which to spiritually educate and evolve their lives.

Charlie's message of love to his granddaughter Courtney taught me something special. There is a divine energy that powers a true, sincere loving gesture, word, or act to not only transcend all boundaries of life, but—much more importantly— to unite them all.

CHAPTER 23

My First Phone Reading

Fear is a universal response that all of us experience whenever we think we are unable to control the outcome of a situation in the way we want for ourselves.

Most spirit mediums I had so far encountered were naturally gifted, possessing a spiritual ability they had developed since birth on their own or by studying under a spiritual mentor. By contrast, I was purely self-taught. This had its advantages, but it also had many disadvantages. Helpful and insightful answers were immediately available to someone who had many years to develop and understand his or her natural spiritual gifts. But that was not at all my reality. While I didn't know whether I was capable of such a feat, I still welcomed the opportunity to provide a personal reading over the telephone.

Before accepting this specific reading, I shared with my client, Rose, that I was honestly not sure if it would be possible for me. As I've discussed several times before, when I am spiritually centered, I view all increasing challenging moments equally; as opportunities to grow and learn from. When I am mentally centered, I view my increasingly challenging moments with a renewed fear of how I will be perceived by others if the information I share is wrong or inaccurate. Yet if I wish to experience a different life offered by my spirit, I have to overcome the resistance of my mental fears. How I respond to these increasingly challenging moments is a great way to validate just how much faith and courage I have in my co-partnership with God. This co-partnership requires me to make a sincere, willful effort on my part while allowing the results of that effort to naturally unfold according to God's will.

I prepared for about forty-five minutes prior to the scheduled reading, which I set for early afternoon. I made sure I was in a deep, spiritual state of peace, quietness, stillness, and oneness. During my preparation, I began to sense the presence of a female child, whose spirit began to show me images of her contorted and twisted young physical body and a sense of how difficult it had been for her to physically and mentally function in a normal way when she had been on Earth. Finally, the young spirit shared a name with me that sounded like either Eric or Erica. (To recap, whenever I received a name, I had to remember that it could represent the first name of a person who was currently living just as it could represent the first name of someone on the other side. Either way, the name is usually meaningful to the spirit, the living relative, or both. If the name belongs to someone who is alive, I receive information or insight about that living person. In this particular reading, I wasn't immediately sure to whom the first name referred.) The young female spirit continued to show me more images of her distorted body, communicating the difficulties she'd had in her earthbound life and the great personal care she had needed from her mother.

At about that point, I paused my communication with the spirit. It was important to share as much information as I received from spirits with their living relatives in real time. I continued to surrender myself to the energetic influence of this young female spirit while dialing Rose's phone number.

After Rose and I greeted one another and I provided her with my guidelines for my readings, I asked if I could share with her the information I had just received from a spirit of a young child. Rose agreed and became silent. Even though I felt confident the information was accurate, I would not be sure until Rose validated it.

I told Rose I had been in communication with a young, female spirit who seemed more like a close family member of Rose's than a friend or distant relative. I explained that the female spirit had been showing me images of when she was a young child, particularly images of her physical body as being twisted and contorted. The spirit had said she hadn't had a long life here on earth due to her physical and medical issues. I explained that the young female spirit had communicated a name sounding like either Eric or Erica.

Before I could continue, Rose exclaimed, "Oh my God!" Rose told me she'd had a child, whom she'd named Erica. Erica was born with muscular dystrophy and suffered multiple physical deformities. The deformities had proven irreversible and, doctors had told Rose that such deformities would ultimately cause Erica's early death. I suddenly felt the need to stop Rose from speaking to allow Erica's spirit more of an opportunity to communicate with me.

Erica's spirit asked me to thank her mother for her many years of help. I received a vision of how difficult it was for Rose to bathe and feed Erica, but the love and care Rose had given Erica was just as apparent. Erica's spirit told me that she now enjoys wonderful freedom without the burden her physical body had once been; that she "forgave [her] mom;" and that she now "understood why." Though her life had been short, Erica knew Rose never wanted anything in return for her love, and from that Erica's spirit had understood what a gift that sacrifice had been. Erica told me that was how angels communicated—by offering their love and guidance without wanting anything in return.

At that moment, I began to sense the communication from Erica diminishing. Before Erica ended our conversation, she asked me to share with Rose how truly helpful Rose had been during her brief life on Earth. Erica loved her mother very much and requested that I once again tell Rose that she "understood."

Taking a moment for herself, Rose was silent before speaking but soon informed me that everything I'd shared made perfect sense to her. Taking care of Erica had been so demanding that eventually Rose felt she had to take Erica to a facility to receive the daily care she needed. The decision had been incredibly difficult to reach back then, and Rose still worried whether she had made the right choice. She admitted to having received several personal readings from legitimate and credible mediums over the years, but this was the first time someone had been able to communicate with Erica's spirit. When Erica had said she "understood," Rose had known in her heart that Erica had been referring to Rose's decision to seek outside care. As a result of the love and insight Rose had received from the spirit of her daughter, Rose said she felt spiritually lighter, as if her process to truly heal had finally begun. After that closing remark, Rose and I ended the reading and hung up.

Again, I returned to my earlier contemplation about how past mental fears had played a major role in preventing me from choosing wisely and moving my life forward. Earlier that day, my thinking seriously questioned and challenged my spirit's ability to communicate with someone's loved one in spirit over the phone. That fear was the result of my brain thinking about and dwelling upon a concern that it (by itself) couldn't control the outcome of this experience in the positive way it wanted.

So far, every moment my thinking has cast doubt on the existence and communication of my spirit, that doubt has proven untruthful. In contrast, the knowledge and guidance coming through my spirit while in a state of spiritual oneness has always proven to be loving and truthful, confirming that this source of wisdom is never something I need to fear.

CHAPTER 24

The Spirit of a Murdered Woman

The level of our own wisdom will best determine our own destiny.

There was a big difference in the number of homicides that occurred within the jurisdiction of the police department where I worked compared to the neighboring jurisdiction of Trenton. Several years could pass in Hamilton, New Jersey, where only a single homicide occurred or even none at all. If it did, it inevitably became the main topic of conversation at the department for quite some time.

One afternoon, a coworker informed me that an unclothed body had been found nearby. It had decomposed enough that the victim's gender was not readily apparent. One or two detectives in the Criminal Investigations Bureau had some knowledge of the spiritually centered existence I was pursuing. One particular detective, Julie, was very supportive of the abilities I had been making an effort to develop. Through her encouragement, I found myself with an opportunity to demonstrate whether I could communicate with the spirit of a homicide victim in effort to come up with relevant information and evidence. I didn't think it would be that much different from communicating with Erica's spirit while on the phone with Rose.

Julie agreed to stay abreast of the investigation to help me with any information I could potentially receive from the spirit of the homicide victim. I decided that my first attempt to communicate with the victim should be at the location where the body was discovered. The only knowledge I had so far was that they believed gender of the victim was female.

Over the next few days, the department was able to establish the victim's personal identity and place of residence as well as a few other minor details. Due to scheduling conflicts, it was difficult for Julie and me to arrange a time to visit the location where the body was found. It always seemed as if some unexpected occurrence, work-related issue, or personal obligation interfered with our attempts.

It was about a week after the woman's body was first discovered that I felt a strong sense to communicate with the woman's spirit. I once again got that "window of opportunity" feeling regarding how long the communication would be available to me. One evening at the department, all the detectives I worked with had either called out sick or scheduled themselves off, giving me the perfect chance to try to communicate with the murdered woman's spirit. After my shift, I secured my office door and sat in a chair. After several minutes, I began to slip into that state of spiritual peace, quietness, stillness, and oneness that I was now accustomed to experiencing. I allowed myself to become aware of any spiritual presence that wished to make itself known to me, especially the murdered woman's spirit. Within a short period of time, I sensed the presence of a female spirit who had a horrific death, so I proceeded forward with great hope that she was the murdered woman, as I wished to hear from her. I spent over an hour receiving messages from this woman-spirit and writing down the information she gave me as quickly as I could. Her messages conveyed several details: a vehicle with an out-of-state license plate, specific types of pets she'd had, the kind of small, run-down home she'd lived in, details about her addictive lifestyle, the abusive boyfriend she'd lived with, how she was physically hit and strangled, and that her boyfriend killed her.

On my drive home, I started feeling hesitant about giving my written details to Julie. Especially when I was tired, my brain was great at inflicting me with doubt. Now it was dismissing the possibility that any information I had written down was at all accurate. After a good night's sleep, I awoke the following morning and reread my notes, yet worry still nagged at me. What if nothing I'd written had any meaning and was all nonsense? I hadn't even been completely sure I'd been communicating with the spirit of the same woman who was recently murdered. Maybe I was communicating with someone else who'd died in a similar fashion, or maybe my mind made it all up because I wanted it to be true.

It wasn't for another day or two that Julie and I managed to meet. When I handed Julie my notes, I asked that she please remember I was new to all of this. My hope was that at least one or two things I'd written down would be accurate and helpful.

The very next day, Julie phoned me and told me she shared the information in my notes with the lead detective of the investigation. Although there were also several pieces of information I'd received from the spirit of the murdered woman that the lead detective couldn't confirm at that time, he was surprised to find that numerous details I'd come up with were consistent with his findings, including how the woman was murdered; that the transportation of her body had been in a truck with out-of-state license plates; details about the kind of home she had lived in and the somewhat unique pets she'd possessed; whom she'd lived with; and the person who had killed her.

After Julie and I hung up, I took a moment to contemplate every-thing I'd just experienced, maintaining my sincere interest to learn more from my journey to be more of God. One of the insights I gained from this and prior experiences is the knowledge that my spirit receives from higher wisdom; a spiritual presence within my home; a spirit over the phone; a specific murdered spirit. or a living person's medical imbalance is all communicated to me in the very same way. For me, the language of my spirit is the language of God. The underlying education of this universal language always points to the communication and power of unconditional love.

I thought about how throughout history, we human beings have segregated ourselves from one another by creating all sorts of different languages by which we'd govern ourselves and our various cultures. In contrast, the "language of God" is quite different; it's something everyone's spirit "speaks"; it does not segregate us but instead unites us with a universal identity. The language of my spirit is best served when my effort to communicate with other spirits is done so with a sincere, loving need to be helpful to God, myself, or someone else. I find it interesting that, so far, I have never had a spirit lie to me—perhaps because spirits lack a physical brain that deceptively and convincingly influences us to not speak the truth or act in a sincere, truthful way. The only time the visionary information my spirit receives seems not accurate is when I am unable to properly interpret those sudden visions, thoughts, or images.

My physical lifetime—as well as everyone else's—is filled with endless opportunities divinely designed to help me self-realize what I must do to wisely live my life. I have come to understand that it is definitely my own level of wisdom that will best determine my own personal destiny.

CHAPTER 25

My First Public Mediumship Gallery

God does not try to prove God's own spiritual existence to people. It is people who need to prove a spiritually loving existence to God.

I was still having moments when my blind faith to follow my initial inner guidance fell short, especially when the guidance I was being inspired to act on wasn't something I felt I was capable of or ready for. This is exactly what I found myself confronting when I was guided to host my first public spirit mediumship gallery.

Putting myself in a situation where I would stand in front of group of strangers who paid me to receive credible and accurate information from the spirits of their loved ones was an enormous step. Giving free one-on-one and small-group readings for people I personally knew or for their close friends was one thing, but there was something very intimidating about accepting a fee. It felt more like a transaction for which I was expected to provide a service that either met or exceeded people's general expectation of my abilities.

In addition, the idea of providing a group reading for two full hours left me wondering if such a feat was far beyond my current capability. The life lesson I grasped on to for comfort was the following: the progressive evolution of my spirit is mostly accomplished by making a sincere, willful effort to act on any spiritual guidance I am receiving because it will result in a loving outcome that I will benefit and learn from.

Sarah had recently been attending events at a holistic center in Plainsboro, New Jersey. The center was owned and operated by a woman named Celia, whom Sarah got to know personally. The center encouraged anyone who wished to hold spiritual events, classes, and workshops to do so, and they could also accept a monetary fee. Celia herself would advertise the events. Through Sarah, I got the sense that Celia didn't allow just anyone to rent space at the center. She made sure the people she dealt with were credible and that what they wished to offer was a good fit for the center.

I knew what I was being inspired to do, yet once more, a closing window of opportunity presented itself. A couple of days later, the compelling spiritual need to call Sarah became quite strong, so I got in touch with her. I asked Sarah how she felt about contacting and intro-ducing me to Celia. Her response was nothing short of the complete support that a true friend would offer. She said she would make the phone call immediately and was confident the reply would be favorable. The next day, Sarah let me know she had spoken with Celia, who said she was very open to the idea of having a new spirit medium hold a gallery at her center. Celia had also said it was important for her to first meet me and provide her with a personal reading. The outcome of the reading would help her make her decision.

When I called the holistic center the following day, Celia's pleasant voice helped ease the nervousness I was experiencing. We scheduled a date and time to meet a few days later. When I arrived, Celia greeted me at the center's entrance. She was a poised and calm woman and spoke with a refined tone. She and I chatted a while about my personal back-ground, my experience, and the intentions I had for the gallery reading. (I'm sure Celia gauged my I'm-totally-new-to-all-of-this sentiment during the conversation!) Finally, the moment came for me to provide Celia with a personal reading. Initially, my ability to receive insight for her simply abandoned me, and I went completely blank. I knew I felt intimidated by what Celia represented for me and what she had personally accomplished. Besides owning a successful holistic business, she was also a certified past-life regressionist, master Reiki practitioner, and certified massage therapist. Thankfully, I managed to find the willful strength to overcome my initial lack of personal connection, and I was finally able to achieve a state of spiritual peace, quietness, stillness, and oneness. I began to be inspired with information about Celia, and I received images about people who were meaningful to her. For about fifteen minutes, I shared my interpretation of the knowledge and images I was receiving. Afterward, Celia's pleasant smile paved the way for her words of approval. I was overjoyed when she welcomed me to her holistic center and her spiritual family of friends.

Celia and I set a date for my first spirit mediumship gallery. She then shared some information with me that immediately validated my initial inner guidance and the sense that my window of opportunity to contact this woman was closing. Celia had been working with a spirit medium who had been providing successful galleries at her center for quite some time. However, just a few days earlier, Celia and the spirit medium had decided it was best to part ways, effectively ending the spirit medium's association with the holistic center. Celia stated that she had been looking for another spirit medium, and I had called her at the perfect time to fulfill this personal need. As I left the center, Celia made a brief comment about "Karma bringing us together." I wasn't quite sure what Karma was or what it did, but I did know that this experience was proving to be a positive one.

My first spirit mediumship gallery was scheduled to take place in just three short weeks. I wasn't fully ready, but I still had time to prepare. I didn't feel capable of switching conversations with spirits quickly enough to provide a large number of people with personal readings in a two-hour period, nor was I sure if I could even communicate with spirits for two straight hours. So, for those three weeks, I arranged with friends to provide "mini-galleries" at my home for a small fee for groups of three to six people. I was hoping if I could learn to provide meaningful personal readings for small groups, I could eventually provide readings of the same caliber for larger ones.

More and more I was seeing how necessary it was for me to do my part to commit myself to the higher guidance being communicated through my spirit, to act faithfully on that guidance, and to surrender control over its outcome. This was my new standard for experiencing my life, and it was becoming more like second nature to me.

I also felt some relief in knowing that I didn't have to provide a personal reading to every single person present unless the number of people that attended was small. My initial goal was to connect at least six people with spirits of their loved ones and share information that was both credible and enlightening to them.

The three weeks passed rather quickly. I contacted Celia a couple of days prior to the date of the gallery to ask whether anyone registered for my event. When she informed me that twenty-one people had registered, I felt ill. She said she was pleasantly surprised that my first mediumship gallery had been received with such enthusiasm, confiding that many of her regular providers' spiritual events do not receive that much attention.

On the evening of the event, Melanie offered to introduce me to begin the gallery. We agreed that her introduction would be brief and that the only thing she wouldn't mention was that this was my first public mediumship gallery. I was concerned that such information could cause an unfavorable response from the group. Summoning the courage and having the blind faith to stand in front of twenty-one people and communicate with the spirits of their loved ones pushed my limits. Holding onto my life lesson—to exist within the moment— kept me centered and spiritually aware. Living in the moment prevents our negative thinking from responding with worry followed by physical stress over future events and situations that our brain realizes it can't control.

Before the gallery began, I spent some time alone in an adjoining room, allowing my spirit to become aware of the presence of other people's loved ones in spirit. I was determined to maintain this level of spiritual awareness as I entered and greeted the group. When it was time for Melanie to begin her introduction, I positioned myself against the door to the event room to listen, waiting for her to queue my entrance. I couldn't believe it when I heard Melanie say, "Thank you all for coming to the very first public spirit mediumship gallery of Rich Braconi." The one and only statement we both agreed she wouldn't say had unfortunately showcased my inexperience! This was certainly not the way I had been hoping to start my first gallery.

Nevertheless, I proceeded to the front of the room. After graciously thanking Melanie for her introduction, I started by explaining what it means to be a self-taught spirit medium and medical intuitive. I followed it up with a brief description of my background, which led to the beginning of the event. I wish I could say the event went smoothly, but it didn't. There were several moments when I temporarily lost connection with the spirits of the audience members' loved ones, although I was eventually able to reestablish my conversations with them. At the event's conclusion, I spoke a few final words of insight and thanked everyone for taking the time to attend.

By doing my part to make this event happen, I learned the importance of accepting sincere help from the right people and that my coexistence with God makes me capable of achieving things I could never accomplish on my own.

Over the next several days after the event, I received many phone calls from people who had attended the gallery and wished to set up dates and times for personal readings. Additionally, through word of mouth, one woman sent me an email expressing an interest to sponsor me in a future spirit mediumship gallery at a different location. I was so inexperienced in this area that I had no idea what "sponsoring an event" even meant! Nevertheless, I could already sense that the guidance within me was directing me to follow up with her.

After receiving equally favorable responses from several people who attended the spirit mediumship gallery, Celia suggested we set dates for future galleries and events. Over the next months, I averaged about six personal readings monthly, in addition to hosting a spirit mediumship gallery once every three months. For the first time in my life, I felt I was becoming more and more aligned with a philosophy that was proving the credibility of its wisdom and guidance.

CHAPTER 26

My Experience at Lily Dale

Never underestimate the power and might of a sincere loving gesture.

In July of 2010, Courtney and I traveled to Lily Dale, New York, for a three-day vacation. Lily Dale is a gated community of certified spiritual mediums who invite the public in for four to five months each year. During that time, the community hosts and sponsors many spiritual events, classes, and workshops to anyone interested in experiencing spirit communication from their deceased loved ones. Also offered are free spirit messages twice a day at a location known as Inspiration Stump, located within a ten-acre old-growth forest called Leolyn Woods.

On our last day at Lily Dale, Courtney and I spent several hours hiking in nearby Rock City Park. After hiking, we went to our hotel room to change our clothes and make plans for the remainder of the day. At first, Courtney was sure there were no scheduled events that would really draw our interest. Then she realized that the second daily gathering at Inspiration Stump began in about an hour. Courtney had never seen me provide a public mediumship reading before, so she encouraged me to participate as a "guest reader."

Sometimes the spiritual guidance that can result in profound moments for us to experience will be communicated through other people. If we have not learned how to recognize these moments as such, we can misinterpret them and fail to benefit from their positive impact on our lives. As I had indeed learned this lesson, I accepted my daughter's encouragement.

Courtney and I left the hotel room and proceeded along the narrow roads of Lily Dale to the entrance of Leolyn Woods. A dirt path led to an open area that can seat approximately two hundred people. After finding good seats, I approached the registered medium in charge of the event. She was very accommodating and added my name to the list of visiting spirit mediums who would be permitted to offer messages during the service. I had been placed third on the list, with about four other mediums scheduled to read after me.

While Courtney and I waited for the event to begin, I found myself getting spiritually connected to a man and a woman who had just walked in together. I sensed they were a couple and had recently suffered the loss of a family member. In addition, I sensed the need for this deceased family member to speak. After the first two spirit mediums presented their messages from the other side, my name was called. I walked with some trepidation to the front of the area and then faced the audience, introduced myself, and shared some insight about how I generally convey the information and messages that I receive.

In spite of my obvious nervousness, I spoke about the spiritual presence I had been sensing before the event began—that of a young man who had been recently killed in a motorcycle accident. The young man's spirit told me he was the youngest of three men in his extended family who had the name of John. I asked the audience if there was anyone to whom that information made sense. The couple who had caught my attention earlier immediately raised their hands. The woman promptly stood up and said she had just lost someone close to her who had died in a motorcycle accident, although his name was Joe as opposed to John. I inquired whether there might be two other men in her family named John, if they were connected to Joe, and if Joe was the youngest. She replied that all of that was accurate. I explained that since the names John and Joe shared the same two first letters, my interpretation of what the spirit was sharing was slightly off. I continued to communicate with the spirit of the young man named Joe, who shared that he had been a mechanic when he was alive. I asked the woman if that was true, and she said yes. Then Joe's spirit said that before the accident, he'd had surgery on his left leg. The woman validated that information as well.

Joe explained to me that his family had made a roadside memorial for him near the site of his accident. Some of the items were red in color, including either a red candle or a hurricane lamp. Joe told me that the month of June was very significant to him and that he had been very foolish in life. At the time of his accident, he had been driving too fast and eventually lost control of his motorcycle, resulting in a head-on collision. With great emotion, the woman again replied that all the information was true. Joe communicated to me that he often observed his family at the memorial as well as strangers, all of whom wept and prayed for him. Joe said that here on Earth, he'd believed he could live his life in any manner he wished, something he knew now was false. The life he'd been given had been a personal, spiritual gift, one he should have cherished and been grateful for. That being said, he wanted his family to know there was an incredible beauty where he was now and that no one there was really "dead." Joe urged me to please tell his family to stop crying for him, that his life was not in fact over but about to have a new beginning. When my communication with Joe finally ceased, I gratefully thanked the attending registered medium for the opportunity to speak and returned to my seat beside Courtney, who enveloped me in a huge embrace of appreciation and love. The sense of pride I could feel coming from her was something I knew I'd never forget.

I soon realized the messages I'd received from Joe were not just meant for the couple but for everyone present. The messages were universal and conveyed the fact that life is a truly unique and personal gift—one we should never take for granted.

When the event was over and Courtney and I were leaving, a couple approached us. The man shook my hand, and the woman offered me a hug; both told me how touching they'd found my reading. They asked if I would be willing to provide them with a private reading, but unfortunately Lily Dale requests that guest mediums do not give readings on the premises. Nevertheless, I sincerely thanked them and said how much I appreciated their kindness.

We also spoke with Joe's parents—the couple I'd noticed at the beginning of the event and to whom I'd communicated Joe's messages. They went over every detail of the messages I'd relayed and confirmed that everything I had shared was true. They had come to Lily Dale in hopes of overcoming their grief, as Joe's death had occurred a little over a month ago (in June, which Joe had mentioned was a significant month for him). Before we parted ways, Joe's mother said, "I can't thank you enough for what you've done for us."

Courtney and I soon arrived at one of the two small cafés in Lily Dale, where we met several other people who had witnessed my reading. One woman asserted that the reading was one of the best she had witnessed at Inspiration Stump that day, and she wanted me to know how deeply the experience had affected her as well as the friends she was with. Another woman, who was a very close friend of Joe's family, expressed how grateful the family was for receiving Joe's messages and being able to know he was all right and at peace. She said the experience would help them greatly in their effort to move forward with their lives, and then she gave me a huge hug.

That's when it suddenly struck me that all of this had been set in motion because of Courtney's encouragement, which put a series of meaningful moments, messages, and experiences into play that I and many others may remember for the rest of our lives. Without knowing her encouragement would have such far-reaching effects, Courtney ended up helping a family in true need of spiritual and emotional healing. What may appear to be a moment of minor significance can sometimes be the initial spark that triggers a series of greater events to unfold, the results of which can hold great meaning and healing for those involved. In addition, I realized that I had given something to my daughter just by trusting her. With this clear understanding of the day's events, I took a moment to hug Courtney close to me and tell her how thankful and grateful I was for her sincere expression of encouragement.

While having dinner at the main restaurant within the gates of Lily Dale, Courtney and I were suddenly approached by a man who introduced himself as Johnathan, a resident of Lily Dale for many years. Johnathan asked if I would be willing to help the Lily Dale mediums provide messages that evening in the main church. He pointed to the church through the window, where I saw a rather long line of people waiting to receive a personal reading from a Lily Dale medium. By my estimate, there were well over 150 people in line! Johnathan explained that as a result of the messages I'd just given at Inspiration Stump, a well-respected Lily Dale medium had asked him to locate me and find out if I would be interested in helping. Additionally, Johnathan mentioned what an extreme rarity it is for Lily Dale mediums to request outside assistance.

As much of an honor as this was, I felt I needed to ask Courtney for her consent. After all, Courtney and I had come to Lily Dale to spend time together, and I wanted her to know she came first in my life. Courtney smiled and gave me her approval. So, for two whole hours that night, I had the privilege and honor to sit alongside the registered Lily Dale mediums and provide messages to the awaiting patrons.

A year later, I returned to Lily Dale on my own and stayed at one of their local bed-and-breakfasts for a few days. After I first arrived, I took a walk around the community, visiting locations that I felt spiritually inspired to explore. It was near dusk when I felt influenced to head to the only floating dock on Cassadaga Lake in the Lily Dale community—a wooden structure with a roof that houses several wooden benches and a table. Watching the sun set over the lake from there was simply amazing.

As I made my way toward the dock, I saw a man sitting alone on one of the benches, fishing. He and I greeted one another, and I began a conversation with him about the fishing in Lily Dale. He said his name was Frank and that he had lived in Lily Dale for more than fifteen years. He typically fished from the dock and other locations, although not as often as he used to. After a moment or two of silence, I was about to share my name when Frank suddenly smiled and said, "I know your name. It's Rich." As Frank's face was unfamiliar to me, I apologized for not recognizing him. Curious, I asked him to please explain how he knew me. "Sometimes my wife and I walk up to Inspiration Stump to hear the messages from the different spirit mediums," he said. "One year ago, we were at the event where you communicated with Joe." Frank said the details of Joe's life and the messages I'd provided Joe's family with had touched him in such a way that he knew he'd never forget my face. "The connection you made with Joe that day was one of the best demonstrations of mediumship I had personally witnessed any certified or guest medium give at the Stump," he asserted. Frank also told me he had spoken with Joe's family later on while they were discussing what they had just experienced. He said that the emotional joy and relief Joe's family received from my communication with Joe had been very healing and powerful for both him and his wife.

Before we parted ways, Frank and I shook hands. "My wife and I often talk about your reading," he said. With that, he picked up his fishing pole and tackle box and began to head home. Just before stepping off the dock, he turned to smile at me one last time and wished me a good night. "Hope to see you here again real soon," Frank said.

CHAPTER 27

What Has Changed about Me (So Far)

Being spiritually successful is not defined by what we do for others but by what we have become for ourselves.

My experience at Lily Dale occurred about four years after I began this journey of self-discovery to uncover the absolute truth of whether I am a spirit; whether a universal loving God does exist; and whether a communication really exists that allows my spirit (me) to receive wisdom and a sense of guidance from that loving God.

During the course of those four years, I disconnected from any unproven beliefs to rediscover who I am. I've learned to quiet my thinking and reestablish my spirit as my main source of wisdom. My mental perspective of whatever I was experiencing shifted to a divine perspective—having an unconditional, loving point of view, including a profound understanding of it. I have self-discovered a hidden communication that was created for my spirit to receive knowledge from God and other sources of spiritual energy. I have faithfully and courageously learned to unconditionally rely on this knowledge, guidance, and insight, witnessing the loving and positive changes it has greatly enriched my life with. I can now spiritually see everyone in an equal way; bypassing their human exterior. I see people based on how spiritually learned or spiritually unlearned they are. I am now much more forgiving and grateful toward people and their actions. My life is now blessed with a continuous growing flow of loving experiences to learn and grow from. I've learned to only speak the truth and act in a truthful way while trusting the change it offers. I am much more spontaneous and less serious. I no longer respond to situations with anger, fear, or anxiety. I passionately pursue whatever I sense a natural love for. I no longer try to control my life; I allow my life to naturally unfold. I now possess a proven wisdom and speak it in an inspirational way. And, my spirit's proven ability to receive knowledge from higher wisdom, future events, spirits, medical imbalances, and past events continues to amaze me and continues to improve. Over the past four years, I have been part of and witnessed more healing experiences and personal miracles than during all my previous years of existence combined.

I would like to point out one of the most significant changes was my spirit's shift toward a more divine viewpoint. I wrote about this in chapter 10, "The Author of Authors." I truly believe that my sudden shift of perspective toward a more divine point of view is a natural shift that will occur spiritually to all people once they faithfully demonstrate a sincere and forever effort to regain and strengthen their coexistence with God. This divine point of view helped me, in an educational way, understand whatever I experienced as if I was viewing it through God's eyes. And, this coexistence encouraged, challenged, and compelled me to choose God's point of view over anyone else's.

Over the next seven years, (approximately eleven years since I began this journey), my life continued to unfold in what I consider a more magnificent way. The personal changes and amazing stories that took place could fill another entire book or two. In fact, as this book is being published, I am beginning my next book. I retired from the Hamilton Township Police Department after I was spiritually influenced and inspired to start a spiritual service business called "Expanding the Presence."

"Expanding the Presence" refers to fulfilling our spiritual purpose to expand the divine presence of God within us. Each year since its inception, the demand for the spiritual services I offer organically grew via word of mouth. I now provide public lectures, classes, workshops and galleries on spirituality at ten different locations throughout New Jersey and Pennsylvania. I have a waiting list of more than eighteen months for a private session. I am no longer in financial debt. I was inspired to purchase a beautiful home that fulfilled many of my dreams and current needs. My ex-wife Michelle and I remarried; she is truly my best friend. Michelle attends (she considers it her part-time job) and hosts of all my spiritual events. She is forever a true source of support and inspiration for me.

My Wisdom and Perspective on How to "Be More of God"

Part Three is in the form of answers to questions that have been posed to me over the last four or so years. I provide this section for three main reasons:

A. *to inspire and empower positive change in your daily life*

B. *to offer you more of a spiritual understanding of what you may be experiencing*

C. *to encourage a love-based philosophy*

Also, given the likelihood that readers may have the same or similar questions, I am hoping my answers offer additional clarity.

1. CAN YOU EXPLAIN WHY THE INDEPENDENT JOURNEY OF OUR SPIRIT SHOULD BE OUR MAIN FOCUS IN LIFE, AND CAN IT BRING US HAPPINESS?

The independent journey of our spirit to be more of a universal, loving God is everyone's sole and higher purpose. God created the communication of unconditional love to divinely guide everyone's spirit toward fulfilling its evolution and transformation of self. Only by demonstrating a self-love toward our spirit's evolution and transformation can a human experience that is based on peace, enlightenment, happiness, and love be attained. In addition, by developing a personal faith to follow only the guidance of what love communicates to our spirit, we can simultaneously experience financial and social abundance. When we allow our choices to be guided by what we sense a natural love for, those choices produce loving and positive experiences for us to learn from. This type of life is much more enjoyable than trying to learn from unloving and negative experiences. Our independent journey requires each person to acquire a more profound understanding regarding how to use the power of love to expand the divine presence of God within him or her. No one else can make this expansion happen for us.

Please understand, we are a spirit, not a physical brain or a physical body. Everyone's spirit has an equal opportunity to expand his or her own coexistence with God. Happiness is a loving response that God designed for our lives. When our choice to follow our inner guidance and wisdom produces a loving outcome for everyone involved to experience, we receive a spiritual response of happiness. Doing this repeatedly demonstrates our capability to experience a love-filled life and, thus, eternal happiness. Temporary happiness is a mental response we receive when our mental wants are temporarily satisfied. This type of happiness can become more elusive as our mental wants become harder to satisfy. The spiritual (eternal) response of happiness also makes us aware that we are doing our part to bring a loving solution to our lives and world. Nothing else can validate our true level of wisdom but the amount of loving experiences and outcomes our personal choices are responsible for materializing. Remember, wisdom is knowledge that can explain God and the power of unconditional love in a universal way.

Pointing our personal attention toward ourselves first instead of others aligns us with a philosophy that is better equipped to fulfill our personal destiny. What we are meant to change and can change is ourselves. Forcing change on others violates God's universal law of free will. Our spiritual journey is dependent on understanding this fact and on concentrating our efforts to be more. Once we prove we have the wisdom to positively affect our own lives first, only then do we earn the credibility and capability to enrich the lives of others.

2. IF GOD HAD THE POWER TO MAKE ALL OF US GODLIKE FROM THE GET-GO, WHY DID GOD MAKE IT NECESSARY FOR EVERYONE TO EVOLVE TO BE "MORE OF GOD"?

Spiritually speaking, the "big picture" will always stretch beyond the limits of what you or I could ever comprehend. First of all, it's not our spirit alone that matters most, but the growth of God's presence within our spirit. Remember, as we are becoming more of God, God's love is expanding and growing too. Part of the bigger and complete picture is the specific pace at which the expansion of God's presence and love within our spirit will occur. And, this pace is different in every person. The more effort we put into understanding what God has created and how it's all interconnected toward serving a universal, higher purpose, the better this spiritual education will serve us.

Part of our education is understanding why God has given everyone the equal freedom to choose his or her own educational pace to be more loving toward self and others. For example, if our mental resistance is stronger than our spiritual will, the pace of our spirit's education to be more loving will be sluggish. If our spiritual will supersedes our mental thinking by being permitted to follow its own inner guidance, the pace of our spirit's education to be more loving will be expedited. Put another way, the rate at which each person's spirit evolves depends upon how effectively the will of his or her spirit aligns itself with the will of God while overcoming human challenges and adversities. During our human existence, the evolution of everyone's spirit to be more of a loving God represents the pace that God has chosen to spread God's own love among all people.

3. CAN YOU EXPLAIN MORE ABOUT THIS PACE OF GROWTH?

Take into consideration that we all coexist and possess a divine co-partnership with a universal God. Through this co-partnership, we are capable of nourishing our own spirit with a "spiritual education" that teaches us a way of living based on the communication of unconditional love. If we lose the spiritual centeredness that we were born with, we must learn how to reestablish our co-partnership with God. To do so, we must first demonstrate our ability to completely surrender sole control and ownership over our lives. When we release sole control and custody over ourselves, we place ourselves in a position to be led by the guidance of love and thus become more of God. This process (the evolution of oneself) takes different lengths of time within each person, which represents the freedom of pace that our loving God has chosen to allow that person to become more loving. The more complete faith we demonstrate in our spirit, the more unified our spirit becomes with God, expanding God.

4. HOW CAN PURSUING AN INDEPENDENT SPIRITUAL JOURNEY BRING PEOPLE CLOSER TOGETHER?

When we decide to live a more spiritually centered existence, we will follow the same universal guidance and inspiration only to make choices that are helpful and loving to ourselves and one another. Money, greed, status, and seeking false recognition from others will no longer be choices that will feel acceptable to us. Love is a higher communication and power that creates complete unity of purpose among all things, including relationships between people. Feeling a sense that our lives are constantly being empowered and helped by other people and through divine inspiration makes lives worth living and experiencing. Remember: It is not wisdom by itself that changes one's life. Change only occurs through demonstrating our faith in that wisdom and hence declaring that it is worthy of our everyday existence.

The personal experiences I shared in Part II serve as a perfect example of this. The reason I had such groundbreaking experiences with healing and loving outcomes for myself and many others was not necessarily due to the knowledge I had gained but to the ways in which I demonstrated my faith in that knowledge as a means of proving its credibility. Witnessing the power from being able to speak knowledge that can universally help any person to be happier, more at peace, and more enlightened has inspired many people to do the same. Keep in mind that being loving in your communication means sharing your knowledge and insight in an inspirational way that doesn't interfere with a person's free will. Infringing upon another person's freedom to choose for himself or herself is a very common flaw in the ways we usually relate to one another. Once we learn that each individual has the same common purpose—to experience life while preserving the communication of love—the fractured unity among us will begin to heal on its own.

Lastly, when we become spiritually centered, we exist in the natural, peaceful state of our spirit. If just for one minute, all people demonstrated a sincere love for themselves by quieting their mental thinking and allowing their spirit's natural state of peace to exist, for that one minute we would experience *world peace*. By simply expanding a love for our own lives and ourselves, we can attain world peace for longer and longer periods of time without changing anyone else but ourselves.

5. WILL YOU EXPLAIN WHAT IT MEANS TO RECEIVE DIVINE GUIDANCE FROM GOD?

Love is a communication created by God to help our spirit navigate itself during its human existence. Simply put, what we sense a natural love for is divine guidance from God. Love is a divine, universal communication that was created to guide our spirit toward experiences and people who are helpful to our spiritual growth. What we do not sense a natural love for communicates to us who and what we shouldn't openly expose ourselves to, as indicated from such divine guidance. What we love or do not love is not a mental decision we make on our own. It is a divine influence that encourages us to make a specific choice without knowing why. Eventually, our faith to align ourselves and our lives only with what we naturally sense a love for evolves into a more profound conversation where knowledge and wisdom is communicated to us through inspired visions, images, words, and thoughts.

6. CAN YOU TELL ME MORE ABOUT HOW FOLLOWING MY DIVINE GUIDANCE CAN HELP ME IN LIFE?

Remember, the evolution of our spirit to be more of God is our life and our purpose. Keeping this as our priority while we maneuver among our societal, professional, and social responsibilities is very important. There is a big difference between satisfying our mental wants and satisfying our spiritual needs. To allow God's guidance to navigate our lives for us, we must first demonstrate complete and unconditional faith in what we spiritually sense a natural love for and allow that guidance to navigate change within our lives and to ourselves. The communication of love and our spirit work hand-in-hand with each other. Love is our divine guidance and our spiritual will possesses a driving strength to fulfill whatever our spirit is being divinely guided to do. This driving spiritual strength is commonly referred to as "passion." Passion is an assertive spiritual force that can empower us with the necessary physical strength and endurance to fulfill whatever we spiritually sense a sincere, loving need to do. By following your divine guidance, you are given the necessary spiritual will and strength to overcome any adversities while fulfilling your task. To assist you in understanding what you do have a natural love for, first focus on what you don't have a natural love for (via the process of elimination).

Our divine guidance has the power to help satisfy all aspects of our spiritual, personal, and professional lives. This is not true about our mental wants, however. By surrendering ourselves to what we have a natural love for, we will excel in rewarding careers, share our lives only with sincere and helpful people, be physically healthier, and speak and act only in ways that create loving experiences while fulfilling our education to be more of God. Involving ourselves in what we have a natural love for will always bring unity into our lives, broaden our wisdom, and make our human existence much simpler to navigate.

7. WHAT HAPPENS IF WE DO NOT FOLLOW WHAT WE HAVE A NATURAL LOVE FOR?

It will guarantee us a life of disarray and unhappiness. Disregarding love's divine guidance steers our lives in directions where we must learn our life lessons from unloving experiences. God gave us the ability to learn from both unloving and loving experiences. It is important to note that we do not need to suffer from unloving experiences to be more of God. Unfortunately, the majority of the people in our world do not follow love's guidance, which creates painful experiences to learn from. Not pursuing a spiritual direction of what we sense a love for causes us to pursue an ever-changing mental direction of what we want for ourselves. The more we pursue our mental wants, we create for ourselves a life plagued by confusion, anger, loneliness, depression, disappointment, and spiritual desolation. We cannot expect to receive internal happiness, contentment, and peace when we do not allow ourselves to be influenced by what we have a natural love for. When we choose not to surrender control to our divine guidance, we are essentially saying to God, "I do not need your help or your love. I can do it on my own." And, essentially God's reply to us is, "That's fine; let me know how that works out for you!"

8. YOU SUGGEST THAT WE SHOULD NOT FOLLOW OUR "MENTAL WANTS"; IF SO, WHY NOT?

Remember, our greatest resistance to attaining a more spiritually centered existence is our thinking brain. Our "mental wants" interfere with our divine guidance of sensing what we have a natural love for and our spirit's ability to seek and contemplate universal truth. Unconditional love is a communication that is always spiritually helpful without "wanting" anything in return for that help. When our spirit receives divine guidance, God is helping the evolution of our spirit by guiding us toward loving experiences to learn from without God wanting anything in return for giving us that help. What God is attempting to educate us about is a philosophy based on the power of unconditional love that we need to make our own during our human existence. What we mentally want may not satisfy what we spiritually need, but what we spiritually need will always satisfy what we mentally want. A big part in the evolution of our spirit is attaining the spiritual essence where our loving purpose, actions or words are never based on "wanting" something in return for them. This loving way to experience our lives will eventually reveal its power and ability to satisfy all our human and spiritual needs without ever pursuing what we mentally want. Being more of God is our natural reward, and nothing else compares; yet all can be received.

9. HOW DO YOU VIEW EMOTIONS AS "RESPONSES" DESIGNED BY GOD TO EDUCATE US ABOUT OURSELVES?

Our human existence is really an education and evolution for our spirit. For now, let me just explain God's higher purpose for creating the

unloving responses (emotions) of anger and fear as well as the loving
response of feeling proud of oneself. All our emotions should be seen as
either loving or unloving responses created by God with an educational
purpose and guidance behind them. Remember, when we are being
unconditional in our love (spiritually helpful) toward God, ourselves,
or others, we never "want" anything in return for the help we are giving.
Now, recall a moment in your life when you became angry at a family
member, friend, spouse, child, or coworker. Did that person fail to do
something that you "wanted" them to do and\or in the way that you
"wanted" it to happen? And, because you didn't receive what you wanted
and/or in the way that you wanted it, an unloving response of anger
or perhaps a lesser response of aggravation occurred. God created the
unloving response of anger to make us aware that we are not fulfilling
our spirit's purpose to sincerely express ourselves in an unconditional,
loving way. Now, apply this understanding toward any moment in which
you or anyone else experienced an unloving response of anger toward a
situation and determine whether your anger was actually a response to
not receiving what you mentally wanted and/or in the way you mentally
wanted it to happen. You will realize that anger is a universal response
that was created by God to help everyone become aware that our current
life philosophy is not based on unconditional love.

Fear is another unloving response that everyone receives whenever
their thinking brain believes it cannot "control" the outcome of a future
situation in the positive way it "wants" for itself. For instance, say I had
a fear of speaking in front of a group of people next week. The truth
is that I really do not have a fear of speaking to a group of people; my
fear originates from my brain thinking it cannot control the group to
respond to what I am speaking about in the positive way it "wants." The
same is true about moments when our brain fears speaking the truth
to someone who is meaningful to us. If we could control how a person
or a group of people will respond to our words, we would never fear
speaking those words. Now, when we surrender sole control over our
lives, we learn to follow the divine guidance of what we spiritually sense
a love for, including what is the loving thing to do for our lives. What we
spiritually sense a love for should also be interpreted as an "inner know-

ing" or "gut feeling" that compels us toward the "right thing to do" or the "strong need to do." By dialing into our ability to only pursue loving words and what we sense is the loving thing to do for our lives, we are simply surrendering ourselves to God's guidance. The inner guidance we receive will never encourage our participation in an experience that will not result in a loving and positive outcome, and therefore, there is never anything to be fearful about regarding this source of guidance. However, when we do not maintain our coexistence with God (by not surrendering sole control over our lives), we often follow a mental guidance that persuades us to make unwise choices that often cause us to experience situations and circumstances that we are not divinely ready for—and that is something to fear.

We all possess the power and ability to greatly minimize (actually, eliminate) the number of situational moments that we respond to with fear and/or anger. The source of wisdom we choose to guide us in life is our most important choice. Realizing the need to only align our lives with the loving guidance and wisdom received through our spirit is a pivotal moment for us. Acting on this realization requires us to demonstrate a sincere faith in this form of communication. By doing so, we quickly learn that our personal faith has the power to strengthen and expand that communication. Our next step is demonstrating the courage in the loving guidance we place our faith in during a moment of personal adversity. By doing so, we will all witness the amazing positive and loving results this guidance foretells. Summoning the personal courage to truthfully act or speak in a loving way during a moment of personal adversity will trigger a divine response of feeling proud of oneself.

10. WILL YOU EXPLAIN A LITTLE MORE ABOUT THE COMMUNICATION AND POWER OF LOVE?

Love is not something that we can give to one another. This is because we cannot give something to someone that he or she was already created with and already has. We can only inspire others with our own demonstration of love and wisdom, which in turn will help them find the spiritual will to expand their own. The communication of love or lack of love always results in an experience that can influence another person's spirit, causing it, much like a sponge, to absorb that loving influence or unloving influence as its own. This is especially true for those who are directly under our influence, such as our children or grandchildren. For example, when we directly influence our children in an unloving way, they absorb that experience and make it their own. Often these unloving experiences can influence children so dramatically that they end up acting in unloving ways toward themselves and, in adulthood, can become self-destructive. When we absorb unloving energy from unloving people, that unloving energy can cause us to be unloving toward ourselves causing us to self-destruct our lives with drugs, alcohol, overeating and other vices.

Wisdom and love are two different things. Wisdom is universal truth that will profoundly explain an unconditionally loving God and our spirit's evolutionary purpose to be more of that God. Love is a power that communicates our wisdom, words, and actions in a spiritually helpful way. Our communication with one another can be imbued with wisdom without being loving. For example, even though the content of what someone says may be wise in that it aligns with universal truths, such content can still be spoken or communicated in a spiritually unhelpful way that results in the content not being received as intended or being rejected. Similarly, our communication can be loving without being filled with wisdom. For example, speaking in a loving (spiritually helpful) way may cause a person to pause and listen to our words; however, if the content of what is said is not wise or universally truthful, then our words will still fall short of their goal. Speaking wisdom in an unconditionally loving way gives our words the best opportunity to be heard.

11. WHY DO YOU FEEL MOST PEOPLE AVOID COMMUNICATING IN A TRUTHFUL AND LOVING WAY?

Most people endorse the mental belief that communicating in loving and truthful ways will not produce the positive outcomes they want for themselves. We begin to operate this way at an early age, a time when we're often influenced by people who are not spiritually centered and therefore not spiritually learned or wise. Those who are spiritually unlearned falsely accept a belief that the outcome of our brain's process of thinking represents our greatest opportunity to receive knowledge that leads to greater wisdom. However, our thinking process is not capable of recognizing, accepting, or aligning itself with a higher wisdom all on its own. Our physical brain needs the assistance of our spirit to accomplish this.

One of our greatest spiritual challenges is learning to disagree with our mental reasons to doubt the existence and communication of our spirit. When we are not taught the difference between spiritual contemplation and our thinking process, we lack the wisdom to choose spiritual inspiration over mental reasoning to guide us in life; and processing our personal experiences can remain very confusing because of this. We can reach a state of mental torment if our stubborn attempts to mentally interpret our spiritual experiences continue.

As I mentioned, when we are influenced by spiritually unlearned people at an early age, we are subjected to a mental philosophy that will consistently seek answers that will give it the greatest opportunity to receive what it personally wants for itself. This philosophy is based on trying to gain control over that which is not spiritually ours, supporting a growing mental ego. (Remember, people are not our possessions; therefore, we do not have control over them like we do our material possessions.) The mental ego offers us guidance on how to get what it wants for itself, even if we have to be unloving to get it. Conversely, when we are influenced by spiritually learned people at an early age, we are inspired by a philosophy that's based on surrendering control over that which is not ours. One of our great life lessons that deserves all our personal attention is knowing what is spiritually ours and what is not spiritually ours. Understanding the difference between these two philosophies is crucial to the real development and education of our spirit.

12. CAN YOU EXPLAIN MORE ABOUT HOW OUR SPIRIT IS CHALLENGED TO ALWAYS BE LOVING?

Our spirit is challenged most when we alter the natural alignment of "Spirit, Mind, Body" to an unnatural alignment of "Brain, Body, Spirit."

This is because our spirit should always be at the forefront of our lives and not last.

Our spirit began its human existence enjoying a harmonious alignment with the physical body and physical brain ("Spirit, Mind, Body"). When we are unwisely taught to use the thinking process of our brain as our primary means to access truth and higher wisdom instead of our spirit, we unintentionally alter this harmonious alignment from a state of spiritual centeredness to that of mental centeredness. The main difference between a spiritually centered existence and a mentally centered existence is the way we interpret what we are experiencing and the lack of inspiration we receive. When we are mentally centered, our lives suffer as they lose connection with our higher wisdom. But when we are spiritually centered, our spirit is very capable of receiving higher wisdom, or a "spiritual education" on loving unconditionally.

13. THE TERM I LEARNED IS "MIND, BODY, SPIRIT," NOT "SPIRIT, MIND, BODY."

"Spirit, Mind, Body" is the harmonious alignment that our spirit, physical brain, and physical body started its human existence with. Our spirit was purposely created to be at the forefront of our lives, and not last, in order to naturally coexist with God's wisdom and loving guidance.

In God's natural harmony of "Spirit, Mind, Body," our spirit has the strength to compel our thinking brain into a quiet state so it can exist as our main source of wisdom and guidance. This places our brain in a less dominant position, preventing it from attempting to interpret life all on its own.

Most people aren't aware that our thinking brain and our mind are two different things. Our thinking process is a result of our brain trying to interpret the truth and receive wisdom all on its own. Our mind is a result of a quiet brain working in harmony with our active spirit. This mindful union comes from God's requirement for our spirit to first receive truth-based knowledge before it shares it with our nonthinking, quiet brain. After our spirit receives truth-based knowledge in the form of spiritual energy, our spirit then shares what it has received with our nonthinking, quiet brain in the form of visions, images, thoughts, and words. This combined healthy union results in a unique communication that produces our *"visionary mind."* Some people refer to this as their *"third eye."*

In addition, when our thinking process is quieted, we enjoy the naturally peaceful state of our spirit. This peaceful state is then communicated to our physical body. When our physical body is directed to remain in a peaceful existence, its health and well-being are no longer influenced by the ill effects of mental stress, frustration, worry, or anxiety. The more our physical body enjoys a healthier existence, the greater the length of earthly time our spirit will have to fulfill its purpose to be more of God. This is the harmonious existence that results from doing our part to maintain the natural alignment of "Spirit, Mind, Body."

14. WHAT IS THE DIFFERENCE BETWEEN WHAT WE HAVE FAITH IN AND WHAT WE HAVE BELIEF IN?

Remember that there are two sources of knowledge our spirit can freely choose for guidance. One is our thinking brain, and the other involves love's guidance and God's wisdom, which is only communicated through our spirit. Belief is a mental possibility, while faith is a commitment to universal truth—the one true religion or spiritual essence that everyone shares. As a result of such a commitment, our spiritual faith will always seek to prove or disprove our mental beliefs in order to ascertain universal truth. Universal truth is knowledge that affects everyone's life in the same equal way, one based on the power and communication of unconditional love.

15. CAN YOU EXPLAIN MORE ABOUT HOW OUR SPIRITUAL FAITH IS RELATED TO OUR SPIRITUAL WILL?

View faith as encouragement that our spirit can communicate. If we place our faith in our mental guidance, we will encourage it to be more dominant; if we place our faith in our spiritual guidance, we will encourage it to be more dominant. Our faith in an unconditionally loving God encourages the will of our spirit to align itself with God's will. Spiritual will is our spirit's strength that we use to overcome personal adversities and resistance, including our own thinking. A good example is the amount of time our spiritual will can keep our thinking brain quiet; reestablishing our loving coexistence with God. Everyone has the spiritual will to quiet his or her thinking brain for a short period of time. In the beginning, I could only manage to quiet my random thinking for mere seconds. The length of time you can keep your random thinking quiet represents the strength of your spiritual will. Right now, I am capable of quieting my random thinking for almost an entire day, every day. By being unconditional in our faith to be more of God, our spirit is encouraged to remain steadfast in its commitment to strengthen its will to do so.

I should note that placing our faith in another person does not guarantee growth of that person's spiritual will to do the loving thing for himself or herself. It is only that person's faith in himself or herself that can strengthen his or her will to do the loving thing. Each person's life is an independent spiritual journey, and his or her responsibility for that journey cannot be shared with anyone else.

16. HOW CAN WE EXPERIENCE LASTING, LOVING RELATIONSHIPS WITH OTHERS?

Lasting, loving relationships with other people are the product of having mastered three main life lessons. The first lesson is that we are all "spiritual guests" in one another's lives, which means that people are not our possessions, and we can expect to receive an unloving response from others if we attempt to "control or own" them. No one was born with an obligation to share his or her life with someone else. How long our "guest" remains in our lives depends upon how much they love the kind of person we are and how much we love the kind of person they are.

The second lesson is that we must demonstrate unconditional love for ourselves first before we can expect to enjoy a long-term loving relationship with someone else. Part of practicing unconditional self-love is seeing ourselves truthfully, which helps us remain humble, which is very attractive. Practicing truthfulness with ourselves allows us to see the changes we need to make to become more of God. Unconditional love is about being helpful to God and others without wanting or expecting anything in return for our help. Helping and adding to someone's life without wanting anything in return is also very attractive. When we can contribute to one another's lives without placing our own spiritual needs second, we are living spiritually free. Adding to the life of another without interfering with our own spiritual freedom is a great recipe for creating long-lasting relationships.

The third lesson is that we must utilize our divine guidance to share our lives with the right people. Knowing with whom to share our lives and with whom not to is a necessary ingredient. No one can expect to have a lasting, loving relationship with someone who follows a philosophy that is self-destructive, causing pain for himself or herself, or toward those nearby. Trying to be close to such a person only sets us up for disappointment and frustration. It can be all too easy to mistakenly believe that selflessly offering our help to someone is all we need to do to get that person to change for the better while genuinely loving us back. Demonstrating a contractual purpose of being helpful to someone in exchange for that person's sincere love represents a type of contract that is often unfulfilled. These types of relationships result in a very low standard of what a true, loving relationship is designed to represent.

Relationships are meant to spark truthful change in everyone involved. When we do not allow truthful change to transform ourselves for the better, we repeat our unwise ways and the negative outcomes they produce. Each person merely demonstrates the level of wisdom and love he or she has genuinely earned, which is passed on through his or her own words and actions. Never allow someone's unloving words or actions affect you in a personal way. A person's words and actions are merely informing you how loving and wise or unloving and unwise that person has grown to be so far.

It is crucial that we avoid interfering with one another's independent spiritual journeys and thus one another's spiritual freedom. Our spiritual freedom to pursue what we have a natural love for and being able to follow our divine guidance are integral to our overall happiness.

The best way to behave in an unconditionally loving way without intruding upon a person's free will is by being inspirational with our words and actions. When we avoid intervening with people's freedom to choose, they experience only the love in our communication. This can potentially motivate them to live more lovingly. For example, without any forcefulness, simply share insight and wisdom that you've gotten from some of your own life experiences. One person's experiences may be quite different from another's, yet any true insight and wisdom people receive from their experiences will always be universal. By simply sharing our personal experiences with others, without being forceful, we create an opportunity to enlighten and empower people. In such a situation, we also give them the space to either accept our insight or reject it. When our words do not intrude on people's freedom to choose for themselves, they experience the love in our words, and that is always enough.

17. HOW CAN I RECEIVE HIGHER WISDOM FOR MYSELF?

Receiving higher wisdom is part of our everyday lives. It is not a rare event at all. We constantly are being inspired with knowledge to guide our lives; but remember, our brain can't receive higher wisdom all by itself—only our spirit can. We cannot receive higher wisdom by existing mentally centered. When we exist mentally centered, the insight and guidance that is attempting to communicate with our spirit goes unnoticed. To change this, we must make a real effort to put more faith in the knowledge our spirit becomes aware of suddenly. Higher wisdom is knowledge that will come to us in a loving way through the power of inspiration.

When we quiet our thinking brain to become more spiritually aware, this event can be so powerful than it can wholly disconnect us from our physical senses, often causing the blank stare of a daydreamer. Creative people such as artists, writers, scientists, philosophers, and musicians who regularly quiet their thinking to allow themselves to be inspired with specific knowledge often find themselves in such a daydreaming state. This is a good sign that they have attained the necessary spiritual state to receive the insight, guidance, or knowledge that they are hoping to receive.

18. WHAT EXACTLY IS SPIRITUAL AWARENESS?

Our brain receives its knowledge by interpreting what the physical body sees, hears, smells, feels, and tastes. By contrast, our spirit receives knowledge by being able to access the same knowledge of another source of spiritual energy. Spiritual awareness is our spirit's ability to sense the presence of other sources of spiritual energy and the essence of knowledge they possess. For instance, I may walk into a room of people and become spiritually aware of (sense) a negative essence coming from a specific person. Or, I may become spiritually aware of (sense) the job, person, or experience that will add to my life over ones that will not. Or, I may become spiritually aware of the presence of a loved one in spirit who is trying to communicate. When our brain enjoys a moment of quietness, our spirit shifts to the forefront of our lives and becomes our main source of communication. This enables us to participate in a mutual flow of communication with all sources of spiritual energy. This is why we are capable of becoming more aware of everything. Our spirit has the ability to direct its awareness toward a specific source of spiritual energy to receive any knowledge that source offers to share. Additionally, receiving knowledge that is outside of what our mental brain is capable of on its own is commonly referred to as *spiritual intuition*.

19. WHAT CHALLENGES CAN I EXPECT TO EXPERIENCE WHILE I AM LEARNING TO BE MORE SPIRITUALLY CENTERED?

One of our greatest challenges is overcoming our brain's mental resistance toward our spirit's existence and communication. As we begin to demonstrate faith in our spiritual voice, moments will occur in which that voice may clash against the voices of those who are spiritually unlearned. As difficult as these moments may be, they are actually wonderful opportunities for us to strengthen our spiritual will.

To attain a more spiritually centered existence, our faith in accepting the knowledge we "sense and know" to be the truth must be steadfast. At first, it is not important to understand how our spirit can receive and access the truth. It is important that we commit ourselves to expanding our faith in this ability. Surrendering our lives to divine guidance and allowing that guidance to alter or redirect our everyday lives is a great demonstration of our blind faith. Whenever we place our faith in the spiritually unlearned instead, we unknowingly accept guidance from a "false God" and allow our lives to be improperly influenced. A false god can be any source of knowledge (such as a person, a book, or a religion) that declares it possesses wisdom capable of helping someone attain a more spiritually centered, loving existence when it truthfully can't.

In situations where the value of our spiritual voice is disputed by social authority, peer pressure, family opinions, or a majority group, we will need to learn how to stop worrying about disappointing others, for our real goal should be to avoid disappointing God and ourselves.

20. CAN YOU EXPLAIN MORE ABOUT THE WILL OF OUR SPIRIT?

We are all born with three sources of strength. The first source, the brain, possesses mental strength. The second source, the body, possesses physical strength. The third source, the spirit, possesses spiritual will, which is the divine power and force that fosters the evolution of our spirit and provides the necessary strength to pursue a more loving way of living in the world. Spiritual will is the force that can quiet our mental thinking, resist those who are spiritually unlearned, and fight harder for what we have a natural love for. Look at your spiritual will as an unwavering assertive force or driving passion that supplies the strength and support to fulfill whatever you are being divinely guided to do. Remember, what you personally sense a natural love for is your divine guidance. Our spirit's will supplies us with the courage to make only those choices that are aligned with God's will. None of our other strengths will help fulfill this purpose.

21. BUT ISN'T EVERYONE BORN WITH FREE WILL, WHICH ALLOWS US TO MAKE ANY CHOICE WE WANT?

Yes and no. The notion of free will was not created by God simply to provide all of God's spiritual children with the opportunity to choose any way they desired. That would serve no real, profound purpose. Rather, God created free will to give our spirit the freedom to learn how to choose wisely for itself. And when we make wise choices, we have loving experiences.

So technically, yes—we can make any choice we want. We can make the choice to be loving, and we can make the choice to be unloving. Yet no—we will not achieve the loving outcome we hope for by making any choice.

22. THEN EVERYONE HAS A SPIRIT—IT'S JUST THAT MOST OF US WERE NEVER TAUGHT HOW OUR SPIRIT RECEIVES INFORMATION?

Yes. Everyone does indeed have a spirit, which was initially born into this world with the natural ability to communicate with God and all other sources of spiritual energy. At an early age, we are commonly taught to place our faith in knowledge that comes from our schools, thinking, other people, books, religions, and our past experiences. Unfortunately, we are not commonly taught to place our faith in the knowledge that inspires our spirit. When we are not encouraged to seek a more profound understanding of how we can spiritually sense or "know knowledge" that represents the truth, our coexistence with God and our lives greatly suffers.

God does not need our help; it is we who need God's help to successfully educate, maneuver, and manage our lives. God does not attempt to speak the varied languages we have developed to divide our cultures. Instead, God created a universal language that governs everyone's spirit that we do need to experience for ourselves. This is why maintaining our natural alignment of "Spirit, Mind, Body" is crucial in understanding the language of God, in the evolution of our spirit, and in creating unity of purpose among all people.

23. IF EVERYONE'S SPIRIT COMES FROM THE SPIRITUAL IMAGE OF GOD, WON'T EVERYONE'S SPIRIT REMAIN PURE?

Our spirit begins its human existence in a very pure state of love, but that purity can be compromised by a spiritually unlearned society and unlearned people. Even though our pure spirit begins its human existence with a natural coexistence with God, our spirit is still required to demonstrate the faith to attain and maintain a spiritually centered way of life during its human existence. God did not create our spirit with all of God's wisdom or love. The point of our human existence is to bring a greater presence of love to our world through everyone's own independent spiritual evolution. Our spirit and the soul of God are two different things, and yet both are on a journey to be as one. In essence, when our spirit evolves, it expands the soul of God within it. The more we are of God, the more our spirit and the soul of God become one and the same. Our spiritual goal is to demonstrate our unconditional love for God, but with the wisdom of knowing why we have to do so.

Let me use the story of Adam and Eve as an example. Adam and Eve were created from the spiritual image of God. Their spirits were created to harmoniously coexist with a human physical form. Even though Adam and Eve had a direct connection with God, they still had to demonstrate their own free will to be faithful to God. When the devil appeared, he falsely convinced Adam and Eve to question and men- tally doubt their spiritual faith in God. Even though God could have intervened to remove the devil's influence from Adam and Eve's lives, God gave them the freedom to demonstrate their own level of faith by letting them freely choose for themselves. The devil did not attempt to physically force Adam and Eve to eat the forbidden fruit. Instead, he wanted Adam and Eve to make that choice for themselves, for he knew that there was no greater way to prevent God's love and wisdom from growing within Adam and Eve than by convincing God's own creation to abandon faith in its Creator! When Adam and Eve chose and used their thinking brain as their source of guidance, a source not directly connected to God, the devil knew he could come up with powerful but false reasoning to convince Adam and Eve to doubt God's word. That is exactly what happened. The devil didn't force Adam and Eve to ignore God's word—their lack of faith did. Adam and Eve merely failed to allow the influence of their spirit to guide them to the truth, choosing instead to follow the influence of a false god.

This story is a perfect metaphor for our spiritual life today. At one time or another, all of us will have to overcome similar personal challenges and confront comparable adversaries. There will always be people who will attempt to influence our lives in a false or "devilish" way. However, the more we accept what the will of our spirit guides us to do, the more of God we will become. As the essence of God gradually expands within us, we will witness more and more moments where instead of some unloving or unwise person having a negative effect on our lives, our loving spirit will elevate its will and wisdom and have a positive effect on them. Despite how pure Adam and Eve's spirits were, both lacked the wisdom to understand that, as we were all made in God's spiritual image, demonstrating our love and faith in our creator was crucial.

24. YOU SPEAK ABOUT EVERYONE HAVING A SPIRIT THAT COEXISTS WITH A LOVING GOD, BUT WHAT DOES THAT ACTUALLY MEAN?

Everyone's spirit was created from the spiritual image of God having the same universal purpose to be more of God. From that creation, our spirit forever enjoys a shared existence with its creator. Formed from our shared existence is a communication that allows our spirit not only to experience God's guidance, but also to spiritually sense the truth and spiritually sense the presence of love or lack of it. At the same time, God created our spirit to exist in a physical body with a physical brain. Having a thinking brain is how God gave everyone's spirit the experience of having "free will" or "freedom of choice." Our spirit can freely choose the source of knowledge it wishes to use to guide its life with, meaning that God's wisdom influences our spirit while our physical brain influences our spirit. Without a physical brain to contribute its "two cents," our spirit would only have one source of guidance to influence its growth and therefore no free will or freedom of choice. One of our spirit's goals during its evolution to be more of God is to no longer experience the will or freedom to follow any voice other than God's.

25. DO ALL OF US HAVE THE ABILITY TO MANIFEST A MORE LOVING LIFE, OR ARE SOME PEOPLE JUST MEANT TO SUFFER DURING THEIR PHYSICAL LIFETIME?

Everyone has the freedom and capability of wisely choosing a loving life. No one is divinely meant to suffer; each individual is merely a representation and manifestation of the level of love and wisdom that he or she currently possesses. We all have the freedom to choose the source of knowledge we wish to guide our lives with. However, not all of us will make the wise choice. Our only absolute destiny is being more of God. The path we take to accomplish this spiritual purpose is up to us. Whether we learn from our loving experiences or from our unloving experiences, we have the freedom to choose which path we wish to learn from.

A couple of years ago, I spoke with a large group of men and women who had lost their children. During this class, I spoke in detail about our spirit's higher purpose and the afterlife our spirit experiences once it ascends from its human existence. I always encourage those who attend my lectures, classes, or events to challenge my knowledge. For me, being connected to a higher wisdom means I should be able to answer anything in such a universal way that all people should receive a more enlightened understanding about themselves, their perspective, and what they have previously experienced.

A woman stood up and announced that she had lost her son in a car accident. She strongly believed she was destined to lose her son specifically so she could achieve a more spiritually centered life. Several other members of the class said they agreed, feeling the same way about their own losses. The woman continued, explaining how she believed everyone was destined to physically die at a certain date and time to fulfill his or her life contract with God and there was nothing that could be done about it. I asked the woman whether, if she had possessed the level of ability to foresee the physical death of her child, she would have shared that knowledge with him, as it could have interfered with his life contract with God. After an honest consideration of my question, the woman said that yes, she would have shared the knowledge with her son in hopes it would prevent her vision from coming true. I then asked those who agreed with a destined-contract perspective if they, too, would demonstrate the same actions as this woman. They all agreed that they would.

I then asked the woman what caused the sudden change of perspective in her. She explained that my question inspired her with the idea that if she had possessed an ability to foresee or predict her son's death, the loving thing to do would have been to prevent him from harm. Instantly, I inquired whether she could recall other moments between herself and her son when she had shared knowledge with him in order to prevent him from minor harm or personal setbacks that were not life threatening. The woman smiled and said yes—she was repeatedly inspired to give him insight to be helpful to him, keep him safe, and move his life forward. However, she confessed, she sometimes chose to refrain from sharing her insight with him because she feared he wouldn't listen, and he would think she was bothering him.

I ended this conversation by sharing the following information with everyone present. I have learned that when we have moments when we are spiritually inspired with insight, advice, or information, a communication is taking place that we need to acknowledge and place our faith in if we wish to help it grow and evolve. This demonstrates a love for ourselves. If we don't, we greatly hinder its growth, preventing this higher-communication insight and knowledge from reaching us when we or someone we love needs it the most. Our intuitive guidance is not only there to be helpful to us; it is also there to be helpful to others when love creates a sincere, spiritual need for it to be heard and listened to. Remember, suffering is not a requirement to learn our life lessons.

26. CAN YOU LIST SOME OF THE DIFFERENCES BETWEEN HOW OUR SPIRIT INTERPRETS WHAT WE EXPERIENCE AND HOW OUR THINKING BRAIN DOES THE SAME?

To begin with, our spirit only receives, interacts with, and interprets truth-based knowledge. Our thinking brain is not capable of distinguishing between truth and non-truth because it is disconnected from reality. As I've mentioned before, our brain receives its knowledge through what we physically taste, touch, feel, hear, and see, but our spirit uses its awareness to be inspired with knowledge that is greater than all our physical senses combined. Our spirit has the ability to obtain the same knowledge possessed by any other source of spiritual energy. Our thinking brain cannot communicate with other sources of spiritual energy on its own. Our thinking brain pursues a path to acquire more of what it personally wants for itself. Our spirit pursues a path that does not place its own will or wants first. Using our thinking brain to seek higher wisdom will often result in a response of mental confusion, worry, anger, frustration, stress, and\or torment. But using our spirit as a means to do so instead will result in a shift of being, understanding, and perspective that will lead to core happiness, unconditional love, simplicity of life, and absolute peace.

Our spirit views everyone in a universal and equal way; our brain views us based on our differences. Our spirit seeks to empower. Our brain seeks to conquer. Our spirit is often forgiving toward itself and others. Our brain often finds fault in others and lastly in itself. Our brain often relives past experiences and attempts to make them relevant to the present moment, but our spirit only considers the moment to be relevant and never the past. To our spirit, success is the demonstration of a universal way of life that is based on unconditional love. Success to our brain is being able to acquire what we want for ourselves even if we have to be unloving to get it. Our thinking brain often wants to change other people. Our spirit only wants to change itself and to do so without intruding upon the lives of others. Our spirit empowers others to be greater than itself. Our thinking brain often belittles others to prove to itself just how great it is.

27. YOU MENTIONED THAT KNOWLEDGE OF A UNIVERSAL WISDOM IS JUST THE FIRST STEP IN OUR SPIRITUAL EVOLUTION. WHAT ARE THE OTHER STEPS?

The first step in our independent journey is indeed to learn the difference between the source of knowledge that inspires our spirit and the knowledge that comes from the thinking process of our brain. Once we have a working understanding of the two sources of knowledge that are vying for our spirit's attention, we can call upon our faith to align our spirit with the only source that is connected to our higher wisdom. Our role is to now accept this inspirational source of knowledge as our means of insight and guidance. We use this inspirational source of knowledge to build upon our understanding of how everything is based on the universal communication of love. As our understanding about the communication of love grows, our spirit will begin to sense a stronger and stronger need to represent this knowledge in our everyday speech.

Verbalizing the wisdom is our second step. Such an act is very meaningful to the evolution of our spirit. At the same time, overcoming the obstacles to do so will present real challenges to our faith. One of those challenges will be to overcome our mental doubts, which will inevitably attempt to convince us that our words do not hold enough truth and wisdom to be useful to others. Another possible challenge is being unable to pick the moments that we speak the truth to someone. Our faith will be considerably challenged when we are inspired to speak the truth in a loving way to someone who will be reluctant to listen to what we have to say. It's important to remember that our main purpose is our own education toward seeing the power that speaking the truth in a loving way has. If we allow a lack of courage to deter us, it stunts our spiritual evolution to be more of God. Take advantage of all the moments that are intended for being helpful and loving. Our efforts may not take root right away; it may take several weeks or months for them to nurture change and growth. Either way, we must do our part. Pleasing others and meeting their expectations should not be our goal; we need to focus instead on being spiritually helpful and unconditionally loving, both of which will ensure a positive outcome.

As a helpful note, if you speak loving and wise words toward others and they refuse to remain open to the truth or truthfully change, then allow those people to drift away. It will only make room for people who are more capable of enjoying a loving relationship with you.

The third step in our spirit's evolution is to change ourselves to demonstrate the universal wisdom we have learned without expecting anything in return for doing so. For instance, we learn that when we quiet our random thinking, we receive a response of "peace"—a "peace" that represents the natural state of our spirit. We learn that this response is not experienced by only a select amount of people but is a universal response that everyone can experience. This universal response is meant to guide and encourage everyone equally toward the proper path to experience a more peaceful and spiritually centered human existence. By accepting that this loving response of peace was created by God to guide and educate us with a more profound understanding of ourselves, we must faithfully explore more of this peaceful state. Knowing this is a path God purposely is guiding us all to take, we must develop the strength to exist in such a state of peace for longer periods of time, even during our daily interactions with others, and no matter what kind of social or professional life we have chosen for ourselves. Committing ourselves to remain in a spiritual state of peace strengthens our co-partnership and coexistence with God.

28. CAN SPEAKING TO SOMEONE IN A TRUTHFUL WAY HAVE A POSITIVE EFFECT ON THAT PERSON EVEN IF OUR PERSONAL WISDOM IS LACKING?

Definitely! The first thing to remember is that God created all of us to be spiritual works-in-progress. In addition, all people are aware of this truth about themselves and others on some level. The second thing is that we were not born with any obligation to help anyone but ourselves, the only exception being any children we choose to raise and guide. (Yet, of course, even children will one day reach an age where they may no longer require or choose their parents' help.) We are each a spiritual student of a life that is governed by the power of love. Our life lesson to wisely choose the right words that best represent the insight we currently possess can be tedious. Our role is to empower one another without interfering with the other's freedom. Even if only a few of our words resonate guidance or insight that is meaningful to someone, we have demonstrated a sincere effort to be helpful. As our own ability to verbalize the growing wisdom within ourselves improves, so will our ability to provide others with the answers that they need to hear.

There is a difference between a real friend and someone whom we are friendly with. Real friends demonstrate the ability to speak to one another in a sincerely truthful but loving way, and they do not have to be all-knowing or wholly enlightened to be a true friend to us.

29. IS THERE ANY INSIGHT YOU CAN GIVE ME TO KEEP ME ON THE RIGHT SPIRITUAL PATH?

- *Place utmost awareness and faith in your own divine guidance and inner voice, and learn to rely on and trust it—without fail. When you support your inner voice, you foster a natural dialogue between your spirit and higher wisdom, or God.*
- *Do not use the random thinking process of your brain as a real source to enlighten your life.*
- *Do your best to be truthful about yourself to yourself at all times. This includes complimenting yourself when others fail to do so. This is your first line of defense in protecting yourself from the unlearned influence of others. Finding your own voice to always be truthful about yourself will not only strengthen your spiritual will but help you remain spiritually centered.*
- *You will always be a spiritual child learning to find your way, and maintaining this perspective about all people will keep you grounded and balanced while being more forgiving toward others.*
- *Make yourself more aware of what you have a natural love for and rely on this divine guidance to nurture the evolution of your spirit. Allow this awareness to change you.*
- *Love is communication that is only experienced through our*

spirit. This communication equally guides all people toward a very specific direction that fulfills their personal destiny.

- *Look at your emotional, mental, and spiritual responses such as anger, fear, happiness, and peace as helpful tools for guiding you toward a better understanding of what it means to be more unconditional in your love toward yourself and toward others.*

- *Learn to walk through your life by living in the moment and enjoying the stillness of that moment. It is this existence that allows our spirit the best opportunity to be inspired with the answers and knowledge that we seek.*

- *Make yourself aware of what is not spiritually yours. Then, give up trying to control those things that are not yours to control.*

- *Always be content with simply contemplating, learning, and changing your own life. Your spiritual success depends on it. Within each person's human existence is a lifetime of universal knowledge that requires our personal attention if it is to be learned.*

- *Lastly, be bold and assertive in what you can expect from yourself and don't be overly serious. Be spontaneous when you sense the spiritual energy to take action and simply enjoy yourself.*

30. HOW CAN WE HELP OURSELVES DURING LIFE'S DARKEST MOMENTS?

We help ourselves by never giving up on ourselves and searching for a more universal perspective to guide our lives daily. Our darkest moments can actually be our most enlightening. We should view the dark moments in our lives as proof that we lack the wisdom to produce loving experiences for ourselves. In such moments, we need to pause and ask ourselves which of our two sources of guidance we have used to place us in such a challenging position. Questioning what we believe is the truth challenges the wisdom we think we have. It not only has the potential to dramatically shift our perspective of ourselves—it can also inspire us to make genuine changes in our lives. When we openly accept that the philosophy we were taught or learned for ourselves is faulty, we are in a much better place to step aside, allowing our inner guidance to take the wheel. During our darkest moments, we are actually in the perfect position to successfully surrender sole ownership over our lives. We're more eager to trust the inspirational answers our spirit can receive and will deliver. By surrendering to our spirit's guidance, we can now accept our coexistence with God and the universe.

Also note that in our darkest moments or any other moments of spiritual need, the help we seek does not have to come from God directly. It can come from any spiritual source of our choosing, such as Jesus, Buddha, guardian angels, archangels, spirit guides, ascended masters, another person, animal spirits, or the spirits of our loved ones. Higher wisdom is God's universal truth that can be spoken by anyone at any given moment. It is not a prerequisite for everyone to choose the same spiritual source to experience the help they need.

31. WHAT IS ENLIGHTENMENT, AND HOW CAN WE ATTAIN IT?

First, allow me to state that experiencing a "moment of enlightenment" is different than being "spiritually enlightened." Having a "moment of enlightenment" refers to our spirit being briefly inspired with knowledge or an understanding that is helpful and adds to our current level of wisdom. If faithful, eventually our few moments of enlightenment will expand into a way of living our lives where existing in a constant state of inspiration or spiritual contemplation is more of our everyday norm. At some point during our growth to exist in a constant state of inspiration, our spirit will develop more of an awareness of the shared presence between our spirit and a God of unconditional love. As our spiritual awareness of God develops, so does our coexistence with God. When our spirit achieves a deepened awareness of God that is more constant than not, we have become "spiritually enlightened." The term "spiritually enlightened" refers to an elevated state of self-being that allows our spirit now to reflect more of God's wisdom and love in everything we do and say.

32. YOU USE THE WORD GOD. WHO IS GOD TO YOU?

God is a divine intelligence, who, through the power of creation, wisely used a governing force based on the communication of unconditional love to influence everyone's life equally while each person pursues his or her own evolutionary purpose to be more of God.

The terms God, the Lord, Yahweh, King of Kings, Elohim, Most High, and the Good are other words or labels that represent the same idea of universal wisdom, absolute truth, and unconditional love.

33. WHAT IS HEAVEN, AND WHAT IS HELL?

When light is present, darkness does not exist. When heat is present, cold does not exist. When love is present, hell does not exist. Heaven is a state of existence where the communication of unconditional love is present and helpful to our spiritual growth. Hell is a state of existence where all communication is based on being unloving and not helpful to the growth of our spirit.

34. CAN HEAVEN AND HELL EXIST HERE ON EARTH?

Absolutely. Heaven and hell are actually a presence of self or a state of existence. They are created within us, by us. When we experience a life with a strong coexistence and co-partnership with a source of higher wisdom and love and have an unlimited freedom to pursue what we have a natural love for, the closer we will be to heaven and vice versa. For instance, if our lives have been filled with unloving people, we may have negatively absorbed their unloving energy. As a result, we might find ourselves feeling helpless, worthless, trapped, angry, or resentful. Such emotional responses, along with the fact that our lives seem lost and hopeless may appear "hellish." Heaven, by contrast, exists in a life saturated with loving, supporting, nurturing, and empowering energy that feeds us with inspirational experiences that fulfills our purpose to be more of God. I am happy to note that our spirit has the power to prevent itself from absorbing or being influenced by any source of unloving energy—for instance, people—as long as its coexistence with

God remains strong and committed. We can keep ourselves in a state of heaven even if we are surrounded by a hellish situation.

The more unloving our lives become, the more we connect it to what hell is like. The more loving our lives become, the more we associate it with what heaven is like. Heaven and hell are merely labels that represent an abundance of love or a lack of love, respectively.

35. THIS IS NOT WHAT I WAS TAUGHT; WILL YOU EXPLAIN FURTHER?

Our loving God purposely gave us the freedom to learn how to make wise and loving choices at a pace of our own choosing. Please understand that God did not make us all wise to begin with. As we learn how to choose a higher wisdom for ourselves, we are going to sin, make mistakes, lose faith, lack trust, cast doubt, be unloving, challenge God, and cause pain to ourselves and others. God knew this, of course. God purposely placed our spirit in a human existence being fully aware we would often fall short while learning to be more. We will not be punished for falling short of what we are capable of because God expected this of us. Remember: our unconditionally loving God does not personally want or personally need anything from us; hence, we are never a disappointment because it was never expected of us to get it all right.

36. DOES THAT MEAN THAT THE DEVIL/SATAN DOES NOT EXIST?

Again, heaven and hell are terms used to describe the presence of unconditional love or the lack of unconditional love, respectively. The same is true for the terms God, devil, and Satan. When we communicate with one another in non-loving ways, we might be referred to as evil or devilish. When we communicate in loving ways, we might be referred to as angelic or godly. Every person's spirit was created from God's spiritual image. Thus, our spirits always possess a divine essence of love that cannot be destroyed or removed—only expanded upon. Pure evil has never existed.

37. IS THERE A DIFFERENCE BETWEEN BEING FORGIVING TOWARD OTHERS AND BEING DIVINELY FORGIVEN?

There's a big difference between our ability to be forgiving toward others and being divinely forgiven. Being forgiving toward others begins with sincerely viewing all people as works-in-progress while understanding that the outcome of their choices merely represents the current level of wisdom and love they possess. Our spirit was perfectly created, but its creation did not make it perfect—meaning there is a lot of room for growth. Therefore, being forgiving toward others as they find their way is important if we are truly wise and loving ourselves. However, it is equally important to know we can be forgiving toward others without feeling required to share our lives with them. Our lives are only meant to be openly shared with people who are open to truthful change. Compassion toward ourselves and others is certainly important; however, we need to cherish our own lives first and foremost and never be careless with them, including in relationships with those whose actions and words regularly convey unloving and unhelpful messages.

We are divinely forgiven for our past choices once we demonstrate an improved spiritual will and ability to make much wiser and more loving choices consistently. A powerful, energetic shift takes place within our spirit when we suddenly choose to surrender control over our lives to speaking the truth and following the guidance of what we sense a love for in conjunction with "being done" with our previous spiritually unlearned ways. When our spirit (which is us) makes and maintains a sincere, willful effort to be more of God, God divinely forgives any past unlearned actions, words, and ways that no longer represent our new, enlightened self.

38. DO YOU BELIEVE OUR SPIRIT HAS PAST LIVES, SUCH AS WITH REINCARNATION?

Our living spirit does not have past lives; it only has one life, during which it enjoys learning from its varied experiences in many different physical bodies during many different physical lifetimes. Our living spirit uses the wisdom and love it learns from its many experiences in different physical bodies during different physical lifetimes to demonstrate the strength to align its will with the will of God until it no longer possesses the freedom to do anything else.

39. WHY DO WE BECOME DEPRESSED WHEN SOMEONE CLOSE TO US HAS DIED?

Mainly, we often feel a response of emptiness, sadness, loneliness, and/ or depression when we believe a source of spiritual need, love, and\or help has been removed from our lives. For instance, any bond of love that is severed between two people or between a person and his or her beloved pet that is preventing someone's spiritual needs from being fulfilled. It doesn't matter if the severed bond of love is caused by death, special circumstances, or personal choice. Each kind of separation can result in the same sort of devastation. Feeling disconnected from God, from family members, or from our real friends can also cause this feeling, as can experiencing the end of a personal relationship or living a life that's constantly plagued by unloving experiences. Simultaneously, our personal perspective of the situation also greatly influences the type of response we will receive when we are disconnected from a source of love. For instance, there are cultures that receive and express a response of joy when a loved one passes. This is due to their personal perspective that the loved one's spirit is now experiencing a much more beautiful, peaceful, and loving existence.

40. IS IT POSSIBLE TO HELP OUR LOVED ONES WHO ARE IN SPIRIT? IF SO, HOW?

You help them the same way as when they were in their human existence. Allow me to explain this to you by explaining my understanding of spiritual awareness, spiritual love, and spiritual inspiration. Love is a communication that creates a shared experienced (bond) that encourages us to openly receive and welcome what others have to say. What we have to say to another can be communicated through physical words, physical actions, or our spiritual presence. The will of our spirit has the power to make itself sense or become aware of other sources of spiritual energy. For instance, if the spiritual presence of God, Jesus, or a passed loved one of yours stood next to you in a room but your eyes were unable to see this presence, your spirit would still have the power and ability to become aware or to sense (they are the same) the spiritual energy standing next to you. The knowledge your spirit received from the spiritual presence standing next to you would be received by your spirit in an inspirational way. Knowledge your spirit receives in an inspirational way will always come from another spiritual source and have a loving purpose connected to it.

Now, when we choose to be a parent, our child is divinely created to surrender to our guidance. Love is a shared experience that forms a unity or bond that God created all children to naturally have for their parents and not just for anyone else. However, if we choose to be a parent when we are not ready, our inability to be loving, patient, and wise to our child can deteriorate but not eliminate that natural bond of love they have for us. Love's power to unite and bond two people together enables their spirits to sense and become aware of each other's presence. Our spirit is very capable of sensing or become aware of God's, Jesus', or a passed loved one's presence in our lives. Now, apply this communication to your child or another loved one who has passed away. When our spirit ascends from its physical body, it no longer has a thinking brain to interfere and resist the communication our spirit is capable of. If my child or someone else I deeply loved passed away, his/her ascended spirit would be even more aware of my presence and every little thing I do. If I had a child who suddenly passed from my life, I would not give up the opportunity or responsibility of being a wise and loving parent to that child. By choosing to be truthful, sincere, loving, and courageous during my own life experiences, the spirit of my child would be inspired with this knowledge and educated similarly— just as if I vocally shared my life experiences with a living child while we ate dinner together. Ascended spirits of our loved ones are very much alive and enjoy an existence far superior to ours. As the spirit of my child would be aware of my every thought and move, my hope of still being able to add to my child's life, by being a better person myself, also remains very true.

God created many different states of existence for our spirit to enjoy and learn from, not just our spirit's human existence. While this type of relationship across two different states of existence (both in a human state with a body that has a spirit and in a state that has a spirit without a body) may not be how we mentally want it, it does enable us to still communicate our purpose to love unconditionally. Remember, unconditional love involves being spiritually helpful to someone without wanting anything in return. This help includes our loved ones in spirit.

41. WILL YOU EXPLAIN MORE ABOUT THE PROCESS THAT HELPS US REGAIN OUR NATURAL STATE OF SPIRITUAL ONENESS?

To regain my natural state of spiritual oneness, I had to start by strengthening my weak spirit. To access my spirit's natural peaceful state, I set aside moments to use my spiritual will to quiet my mental thinking. The process was very slow for me. At the beginning, my thinking brain would assume its dominant role only after about forty-five seconds. Every day, I demonstrated a determined faith to reach and maintain a state of spiritual peace. I patiently accepted any progress that I received. If I managed to quiet my thinking brain for forty-five seconds on one day and the following day I managed to reach fifty seconds, I was grateful that I'd made any progress. I simply allowed my life to naturally unfold without wanting anything in return from God for my effort.

As my spirit increased the length of time it could compel my brain to stop thinking, I sensed that the strength of my spirit's will was expanding and improving. After several months, I was able to maintain a state of spiritual peace for more than an hour, even during daily life activities. To further challenge and improve my spirit's will, I would sit in my living room with both the television and radio on loud and focus on maintaining a state of spiritual peace despite the noise. That experiment brought me to a deeper level that I refer to as a state of spiritual quietness. By totally disconnecting from any outside noise or other distractions, I strengthened the will of my spirit even more powerfully. This greatly helped me in my daily activities by tuning out the noise and the distractions made by other people.

From that state of spiritual quietness, it was easier to receive the knowledge being inspired through my spirit. It became the new standard of how I wished to exist. I began to view most of the world around me as nothing more than a distraction from my higher self. From this, my life pace slowed down considerably and I lived more in the moment than ever. Slowing things down to detect the inner guidance being shared with me was crucial.

It was by living more in the moment that I then discovered how to exist in a state of spiritual stillness, where I strongly sensed my union with all other sources of spiritual energy. I realized that spiritual energy itself exists as a state of stillness, which I was now more a part of than ever.

Eventually, I discovered that when I attained a state of spiritual stillness and opened my awareness to receive insight into what it meant to be more of God, I received higher knowledge through visions, ideas, words, and epiphanies that answered my prayers for help and guidance. I knew I had finally reached the state of spiritual oneness, which enables the spirit to know what God knows and thus access the same knowledge as any other source of spiritual energy. In a state of spiritual oneness, communication is established in a loving and inspirational way. This is now my standard state of existence as I live my life. Seeking the deeper truth surrounding any knowledge we receive from this state adds to the evolution of our spirit to be more of God.

42. ARE YOU AWARE OF ANY SCIENTIFIC EVIDENCE THAT VALIDATES OR SUPPORTS THE SPIRITUAL GROWTH THAT YOU SAY HAS SIGNIFICANTLY CHANGED YOUR LIFE FOR THE BETTER?

Yes. In July 2018, Leigh Povia from the Center of Dynamic Growth in Hamilton, New Jersey, performed an electroencephalogram (EEG) to access my brain's activity during both when I am communicating with spirits and when I am not. Leigh is a New Jersey-licensed clinical social worker, a registered play therapist, an approved EMDR consultant, and a board-certified neurofeedback provider. The test was conducted with my eyes closed and with my eyes open. After the test was completed, Leigh sent the results off to Dr. Glenn Weiner, PhD, to be fully analyzed. Dr. Weiner, of Dominion Behavioral Healthcare in Richmond, Virginia, is a licensed clinical psychologist and is board certified in neurofeedback. After analyzing all the data changes from the experiment, Dr. Weiner emailed me the following comments:

> Hi Rich,
>
> I will be very happy to go over all of this with you when we both find the time. I utilize QEEGs as one of my major tools for understanding brain functioning in my role as a psychologist who does EEG biofeedback, also known as neurofeedback. I have been doing this work for quite some time, and over the last few years have been teaching a class on QEEG and neurofeedback at our international conference (ISNR).
>
> My intention was to be a skeptical observer and see what the data had to say. There were two questions that I had about this. Is Rich's brain functioning different than others regularly? And, is his brain different than others when "connected in spirit"?
>
> Similar to our typical clinical work, we record a ten-minute sample of EEG with eyes open and again with eyes closed. When findings are seen in both conditions, it adds to the validity. In this case we did four samples: eyes closed and eyes open, and again eyes closed and eyes open "connected in spirit."
>
> There is a large amount of data in doing these analyses with the clearest and most understandable being the absolute

power Z scores. This is a measure of the amplitude or power of a particular EEG band. A Z score is a measure of how different a score is in comparison to a normal database.

Rich's data reveals that when relaxing he makes much more 7–9 HZ activity throughout his brain than most others. This is the border between Theta and Alpha. Some people define this as the border between conscious and unconscious processing. When "connected in spirit," his brain functioning is significantly different than when relaxing, and significantly different from other individuals in my database. He shifts into making very high levels of global Delta and Theta as well as excessive Alpha. He makes more frontal Delta and Theta than 98% of the population. These slow waves of Delta and Theta are synchronous (hypercoherent) or coordinated. These findings are pretty consistent across the eyes-closed and eyes-open conditions, which adds to their validity.

Interpreting what this all means is much more complicated and perhaps unknowable. We typically make Delta waves when we are sleeping. Theta occurs in very deep meditation or when very drowsy. Rich is able to somehow quickly shift into these very deep states to "communicate to spirit", essentially at will. A different way to say this is that he is able to enter a different state of consciousness than being simply awake or asleep. How he does this, and how he uses this state is his gift, and makes exploring this so fascinating!

My Closing Thoughts

The most important thing I continue to discover about myself is that "I am" a spiritual being evolving to "be more of God," and it is necessary to live my life as such. A universal God of great love truly exists and can be equally self-discovered whenever a person faithfully uses a philosophy that is based on the communication of unconditional love to build his/her life on.

I have learned that spiritual energy is life energy, which is God energy. All sources of spiritual energy (people) are created to be part of a universal communication that can tap into God's energy and wisdom to profoundly expand themselves. This universal communication has a specific language that only our spirit can interpret by itself. I have used the last eleven years of my life to better understand this God-created universal language. The education I have received from being a student of this language of God has no equal. Even though others may view my ability to communicate with higher wisdom (God), spirits, animals, ascended masters, and angels and to see medical imbalances, past lives, or future events as a divine gift or special ability, I am completely certain it is not. This divine communication created within everyone's spirit goes unnoticed due to our lack of spiritual education and lack of sincere effort to live a more spiritually centered existence. The purpose of expanding on this divine communication within me was not to provide spiritual services for other people but to nourish and nurture my own life. The education I received from faithfully pursuing this universal truth is responsible for the constant state of spiritual happiness I now wake up to.

I have learned that God has the power of creation. As a spiritual child of that God, we have a similar but much smaller power through which our spirit can create and expand the amount of love within itself and inspire love to expand in whatever it touches. God's power of creation and our ability to create more love within ourselves, among our relationships, and between our spirit and God all have the same purpose and outcome: to make something more spiritually appealing and beautiful than it previously was. In applying this power to my life, my goal is to maintain a love for myself while making anything I do or pursue more appealing or beautiful than it was previously. This goal is simple to understand but very challenging to demonstrate. The communication of our spirit exists; trust it unconditionally, place all your faith in it, and allow it to change and transform you. Even though the world we currently live in distracts, doubts, and interferes with people who are learning to live spiritually centered, never allow it to minimize what your spirit is capable of; I say challenge accepted. Always educate yourself with what is universally truthful, speak that education, and allow that education to guide you in life; this is how the people, opportunities, and circumstances that are right for your life will find you. Any other path will pale in comparison. Allow yourself to be amazed and enlightened at the personal miracles your coexistence with God is capable of working together. Never settle to share your life with people, places, jobs, or experiences that you do not spiritually sense a natural love for. The kind of life you create for yourself is your only real and true possession. It is also a testament and validation to the source of wisdom and philosophy you chose to guide your life with. Learn and understand how to make wise choices; it is an endeavor you will be proud that you succeeded at. Commit yourself to being more loving toward yourself. Remember, only your own life is yours to change and only inspire others to change for themselves. Keep yourself balanced by caring without caring too much and never take whatever you or someone else is experiencing too seriously. Our spirit will never experience death, only different life experiences. We will all one day truthfully look upon what we accomplished and what we didn't accomplish during our human existence. Hopefully we will all be proud of what we see. Our human existence is about creating something more spiritually beautiful than what we started with. Our life's work of art should begin and end with ourselves. Discard whatever poor and unloving philosophy you learned from your parents, family, friends, society, or education, so it is never duplicated. Our greatest opportunity to greatly improve our coexistence with one another and our world is by educating and empowering our children to become wiser and more loving than ourselves. And, if this empowering, loving attitude is applied toward future generations, then a more unified existence for everyone to enjoy and prosper occurs by simply *"being more of God."*

Made in the USA
Middletown, DE
07 June 2019